IM POSSIBLE PLANNING GUIDE

Permission Slip

Before you begin using your Self Care Planning Guide you must give yourself permission to make the changes you want and experience the growth you deserve in your life.

Change, even when purposeful is hard. It is also multifaceted. You must give yourself permission to experience and explore all the elements that allow for lasting change, transformational growth and authentic joy.

Permission for acceptance

Acceptance says you acknowledge and embrace that you are not on the path you intended to be. Maybe you got a little lost. Maybe you got a little too busy to nurture yourself and a positive relationship with yourself. That is OK. Accept that. Below write yourself a brief statement of permission allowing yourself to own that you're not where you want to be.

Permission to be imperfect.

What is perfect? Your definition of perfect may be imperfect to someone else. Strive instead to achieve happiness and greatness through acts of kindness to yourself and others. Use this planning guide to help you grow into a person who is perfectly happy, perfectly healthy and perfectly at peace. Use the space below to give yourself permission to grow into a definition of success and perfection that suits YOU, YOUR goals, and ONLY supports YOUR happiness and wellbeing.

Permission to feel

As you work through this planning guide you may stumble across some things you haven't allowed yourself to feel or heal from. Use the space below to give yourself permission to feel those emotions. Internal bleeding far more dangerous than open wounds, scars and vulnerability. Let it out.

Permission to choose

Simply put, if something is harming more than helping or healing, you are allowed to choose to let that thing, habit or person go. This also applies to people pleasing. Give yourself permission to break plans, refuse plans, or say no to anything that doesn't fit your self- care needs that day, week or even month. Use the space below to give yourself permission to choose what activities, habits and people you allow into your life.

Permission to take it slow

It is often said that the best things in life are right outside our comfort zone. Rather than diving head first into the unknown, unequipped just because happiness MIGHT be on the other side of your comfort zone, give yourself permission to take it slow, take baby steps and try new things if they appear safe and in alignment with your goals. It is OK to take your time and expand your comfort zone little by little. Use the space below to give yourself permission to champion your own safety while still exploring new ideas, people, places, and activities.

Anything else?

What permission are you waiting for? What can you give yourself permission to do right now? Give yourself that permission in the space below

The best way to practice self-care is to practice self-discovery. In order to know how to care for yourself, you must know yourself.

Have you ever seen someone you love walking towards you from a distance and without seeing their face know who it is just by their walk? When we love someone, we learn every little thing about them. We learn their mannerisms, their voice inflections, their little idiosyncrasies' that make them unique. We know their walk even from a mile away.

The I'm Possible Self-Care Planning Guide will help you know yourself just as well as you know someone you love—because by the end of this book you will be the most loved person in your own life.

Even at a distance, on days when you feel detached, lost or unsure of your truth, you will be able to recognize yourself, your needs and all the tiny little things that make you unique, capable and worthy of your own love.

WHO AM I?

Welcome to the I'm Possible Planning Guide! Before you dive in, take a minute to consciously acknowledge and celebrate who you are at your core. By purchasing this guide, you have embarked on a journey to become more self-aware, to thrive, to truly love yourself and fulfill your limitless potential.

I AM PERSON WHO….

Loves

Celebrates

Wants to

Believes in

Strives to

Is inspired by

Is happiest when

Is challenged by

Is moved by

will one day

SELF CARE ASSESSMENT

You may have heard the saying "You cannot pour from an empty cup." Before you get started with your I'm Possible Planner, let's take a look at your cups.

There are six elements of self-care.

PHYSICAL: Movement. Nutrition. Health.

PERSONAL: Relationships with self and others

SPIRITUAL: Listening to an inner voice and universe.

EMOTIONAL: Mindfulness and positive Self Talk

PROFESSIONAL: Work/Life balance.

PSYCHOLOGICAL: Self Reflection & Self Awareness

Most of us have been taught in order to be happy each cup must be full. This is untrue. Happiness, peace, abundance and fulfillment come from understanding which cup to fill and when to fill it.

.

If you are filling the wrong cups you may feel full but you will never feel nourished.

What nourishes you will change. As you move through life your needs will change. What fills and fuels you will change.

But before you jump in, let's look at where you are right now. Take a few minutes to write out all the things that fill your cup. Include words, lyrics, people, places, experiences--all of the things that fill your cup. Include both the GOOD and the BAD (yes, sometimes we fill our cup with bad stuff too like negative self-talk, toxic relationships, false comparisons, etc.)

What Is in My Cup

PROFFESIONAL	
PERSONAL	
SPIRITUAL	
PHYSICAL	
PSYCHOLOGICAL	
EMOTIONAL	

DOWN THE DRAIN

Ok, now let's dump. Take a hard look at your cups and on these pages dump out anything you feel is not nourishing you. Some cups will have a many, some may have none. Be honest with yourself. Be kind to yourself and use this as an opportunity to really examine what people, places, thoughts, activities and choices may be harming you.

What is in your cup and does it belong there?

PHYSICAL

EMOTIONAL

PERSONAL

PROFESSIONAL

SPIRITUAL

PSYCHOLOGICAL

Liberation Letters

Use this template to write a letter to someone or something you must release in order to move forward. This letter is meant for you to acknowledge the people, habits or activities that are no longer serving you. Use this template once a month to allow for optimal growth. Use this page or a separate sheet of paper to allow for thoughtful responses.

Dear,

I am choosing to say goodbye because

You should know saying goodbye makes me feel

I would like to thank you for showing me

Because of you I learned

I am now

Because of you I now value

When I release you I will no longer

Sincerely,

How did writing that letter make you feel? This was your first Liberation Letter of the I'm Possible Self-Care Planning Guide. You will complete one letter each month.

Consider why you chose this as your first release. What about this person, habit or thing made it stand out in your heart and mind as the first to go?

You already possess the power to change your life. You hold the power to thrive, to live abundantly and to flourish emotionally, finically and personally. The proof of this rests in your first goodbye. Your heart, mind and soul already know what it needs.

HELLO LETTER

Now that you have released someone or something that has been holding you back from taking care of yourself and living abundantly, you must check in with yourself. This step is crucial as it will promote healing, create a plan to truly move forward and aid in closure. Use template once a month to allow for optimal growth. Use this page or ideally a separate sheet of paper to allow for thoughtful responses.

Dear,

I just said goodbye to

Saying goodbye to makes me feel

but I know it is for the best. Some of the reasons I know this is for the best are because

Moving forward will be hard. That is ok. Please allow yourself time to feel

Some things you can do when you feel upset about closing this chapter are

Some people you can talk to are

There will be ups and downs, good days and bad days. That is part of difficult change, and it is normal and OK. On the really hard days a reminder you can use is

On the really great days a reminder you can use is

Here are three things I feel confident I can do to move forward and say goodbye

1.

2.

3.

Lastly, thank you for acknowledging it was time to let go. Thank you for honoring your health and your spirit. You deserve the best life has to offer and I am proud of you for putting yourself first.

Love always,

WEEKLY WHY

Using this guide, you will be given time every week to learn, grow and powerfully understand your thoughts and decision-making processes.

The formula is simple.

Think of something during the week that excited you, upset you, stressed you out, made you inexplicably happy, or devastatingly sad. This could be an event, a choice, or even a conversation.

Then ask yourself WHY three times. Doing this activity weekly will give you deeper insight into what things bring you ultimate joy subsequently leading you back to truest self and deepest needs.

Example: "I was really angry with my husband because he didn't help me with the chores this week.

WHY: Because that is incredibly inconsiderate

WHY: because he doesn't appreciate how hard it is to keep this house clean and tidy. I am overwhelmed

WHY: because he has never had to do it. He is at work all day and overwhelmed with his own stuff. He is dealing with his own stress and can't relate to mine.

How this works? The first response typically comes from the brain, the second from the heart (emotion) and the final from gut. From the final response brainstorm some solutions.

Example: He doesn't mean to be inconsiderate. He doesn't understand how I feel. I need to communicate that I am overwhelmed and see how we can work together to get chores done and find more time for stress relief. I also could try to support his needs to de-stress a little better. We both have a lot on our plates that neither of us understand. We could probably check in with each other's emotion more.

ANOTHER WAY TO USE THIS FORMULA:

An example of something joyful that occurred:

"I had the best time just sitting at my friend's house talking and watching trashy TV. She made really great food for us and we laughed a lot"

WHY: I had fun because I was with my friend

WHY: I really enjoy spending time with her in particular because I feel like I can be myself with her. I also love that she makes good food. I have been trying to eat better and explore different cuisines. I feel supported in that goal when I am with her

WHY: I am on a journey to find what brings me happiness and nurtures my soul and by spending that time together I realized I need to nurture my friendships more because they make me feel happy and alive. I also should spend more time with the people who have the same goals as me. I need the support and comradery right now.

YOUR WEEKLY WHY

Use this space to learn, grow and powerfully understand your thoughts and decision-making processes. Do this anytime you need clarity. Write it on a napkin, a back of an envelope, a journal, or anywhere you can write down and work through your thoughts.

The formula is simple.

Think of something during the week that excited you, upset you, stressed you out, made you inexplicably happy, or devastatingly sad. This could be an event, a choice, or even a conversation.

Then ask yourself WHY three times.

HOW TO USE YOUR SELF CARE PLAN

Each week you will have the opportunity to JUST plan self-care. One of the reasons so many of us struggle with self-care is that it is simply easy to overlook or feel overwhelmed by. When, between the 9 million other things you are doing will you possibly find time for self-care? Just as you make plans with friends, think of this part as making plans with yourself.

First you will brainstorm all of your needs for the week on the "**My Needs for the Week**" page and then rank by priority.

Next, using the **IM POSSIBLE SELF CARE PLANNER** choose something in each category to schedule in, or just in the self-care category you have determined requires your focus. Make the plan, keep the plan. Just as you would with a date with a friend.

Don't overthink this. Choose manageable goals for each day. EMPOWER YOURSELF with realistic goals you can enjoy and feel good about. They can take 30 seconds like repeating a mantra or 2 hours like attending an event.

If you get stumped, here are a few ideas (ALSO REFER TO MONTHLY SELF CARE TIPS FOR INSPIRATION)

PHYSICAL: Go for a walk, try a new sport or workout regimen, stretch, get more rest, amend diet, run.

PROFESSIONAL: Set goals, set timelines, use vacation day, ENJOY your lunch break, advocate for yourself, take short breaks.

EMOTIONAL: Say YES to yourself, listen to your body, meditate, unplug, cry, have a difficult conversation, random acts of kindness, play!

SPIRITUAL: Learn about moon cycles, buy a crystal, yoga, practice releasing negative energy and thoughts, talk to God or higher power you believe in, learn about your heritage and connect with family and memories.

EMOTIONAL: Stop negative self-talk, notice and cease self-sabotaging behaviors, write yourself love notes, put an affirmation on a post it where you can see it, let go of a toxic memory and/or person or habit.

PERSONAL: Call a friend, meet new people, challenge yourself, be silly, network, attend an event,

MY NEEDS THIS WEEK

Brainstorm your needs this week. Prioritize by number and add to your weekly calendar.

PERSONAL NEEDS:

PROFESSIONAL NEEDS:

SPIRITUAL NEEDS:

PHYSICAL NEEDS

EMOTIONAL NEEDS

PSYCHOLOGICAL NEEDS

IM POSSIBLE SELF WEEKLY SELF CARE PLAN

	MONDAY	TUESDAY	WEDNESDAY	THURSDAY	FRIDAY
PERSONAL					
PROFESSIONAL					
SPIRITUAL					
EMOTIONAL					
PHYSICAL					
PHYSICAL					

Reminders are personal mantras to be used in times of stress, decision-making, or in moments of gratitude and joy. Write your reminder for the week.

Support: Who or what will support you this week in your Self-Care goals.

REMINDERS	SUPPORT

WEEKEND SELF CARE PLAN

PERSONAL	
PROFESSIONAL	
SPIRITUAL	
EMOTIONAL	
PHYSICAL	
PSYCHOLOGICAL	

<u>WEEKLY SELF ESTEEM CHECK IN</u>

Choose 1 of the following prompts to respond to for each day of the week

SOMETHING I DID WELL WAS	I FELT PROUD WHEN
SOMETHING I DID FOR SOMEONE ELSE	I TRIED
SOMETHING I DID FOR MYSELF	I FELT GOOD ABOUT MYSELF WHEN
I HAD A GOOD EXPERIENCE WITH	I LEARNED
I ACCOMPLISHED	I CHALLENGED MYSELF TO

MONDAY:

TUESDAY:

WEDNESDAY:

THURSDAY:

FRIDAY:

SATURDAY:

SUNDAY:

Value yourself.

Appreciate yourself.

Respect yourself.

Believe you are worth it.

It is OK if you are scared.

It is OK if you are unsure

It is OK to have days filled with doubt

But no matter what, in your heart you must believe you are worthy. **The universe will only give to you what you believe you deserve.**

What do you believe you deserve? Write down 5 things you believe you deserve.

SELF LOVE GROCERY LIST

As you create your grocery list for the week try to incorporate at least one food into each of the following categories to ensure you are taking care of your whole body, mind, and spirit. Plan your trips to the grocery store not just for food to eat but rather food that nourishes you. Under Meal Challenge-- think of a recipe you have been wanting to try, a food you want to cut out or add in to your diet. Do this weekly to see a drastic change in your overall health.

BRAIN FOOD	GUT HEALTH
SKIN AND HAIR CARE	SLEEP
HEALTHY INDULGENCES	HEALTHY MUNCHIES
HOUSEHOLD	MEAL CHALLENGE

Recipe inspiration this week (seen on social media, in cookbook, or even at restaurant):

What might my body need the most of this week?

What may throw me off track eating for my body's needs this week? Is there anything I can do to help myself when that happens?

GROCERY LIST CHEAT SHEET

REST

Popcorn, oatmeal, or whole-wheat crackers with nut butter are all good choices. Try popcorn sprinkled with Everything bagel seasoning for a savory treat or dusted with cayenne for a kick!

Go nuts for nuts! Almonds and walnuts, specifically, contain melatonin, a hormone that helps to regulate your sleep/wake cycle. Eating these nuts regularly can increase melatonin in your system, helping you sleep more soundly.

Cottage Cheese packs a punch with the amino acid tryptophan, which may increase serotonin levels. Serotonin is a brain chemical and low levels of it can contribute to insomnia.

A Cup of Bedtime Tea

Certain fruits that contain melatonin may help you fall asleep faster and wake up less often during the night. Tart cherry juice contains a lot of melatonin, bananas, pineapple, and oranges are also fantastic sources.

2 Kiwis one hour before sleep can help improve sleep quality.

GUT HEALTH

Cabbage

Asparagus

Pickled Veggies (and pickles)

Flaxseed

Bananas

Apples

Garlic

BRAIN FOOD

Antioxidants, such as flavonoids or vitamin E

B vitamins

healthful fats

Omega fatty acids

Oily Fish-Salmon, Tuna

Berries

Avocados

Eggs

Vitamin E rich nuts: Almonds, sunflower seeds

Flax Seed

Chia Seed

Cruciferous Vegetables: Brussel Sprouts, bok choy, cabbage, kale

SKIN NOURISHMENT

Tomato

Carrot

Avocado

Eggs

Walnuts

Bell Peppers

Kale

LET'S GET STARTED

Now that you have had a chance to get familiar with this Self-Care Planning Guide, let's dive into it!

Are you ready to begin the process of changing your life?

Last thing before you take this HUGE step into your greatest potential, creating a deep loving relationship with your truest self, and living a healthy, abundant life

- Write down ONE GOAL for yourself for the duration of the year you use this planning guide.

- Use the remainder of this and following page to create a vision board. Do this using doodles, words, cut out from magazines, books...anything that will help you visualize the goal for yourself and how your life and spirit will be as you, and once you, achieve it.

Vision Board

MY NEEDS THIS WEEK

Brainstorm your needs this week. Prioritize by number and add to your weekly calendar.

PERSONAL NEEDS:

PROFESSIONAL NEEDS:

SPIRITUAL NEEDS:

PHYSICAL NEEDS

EMOTIONAL NEEDS

PSYCHOLOGICAL NEEDS

IM POSSIBLE SELF WEEKLY SELF CARE PLAN

	MONDAY	TUESDAY	WEDNESDAY	THURSDAY	FRIDAY
PERSONAL					
PROFESSIONAL					
SPIRITUAL					
EMOTIONAL					
PHYSICAL					
PHYSICAL					

Reminders are personal mantras to be used in times of stress, decision-making, or in moments of gratitude and joy. Write your reminder for the week.

Support: Who or what will support you this week in your Self-Care goals.

REMINDERS	SUPPORT

Healing doesn't mean the damage never existed. It doesn't mean you were never hurt. Healing means the damage no longer has control over your life.

What would you like to heal from?

What are some things you can do to begin the healing process?

WEEKEND SELF CARE PLAN

PERSONAL	
PROFESSIONAL	
SPIRITUAL	
EMOTIONAL	
PHYSICAL	
PSYCHOLOGICAL	

WEEKLY SELF ESTEEM CHECK IN

Choose 1 of the following prompts to respond to for each day of the week

SOMETHING I NOTICED ABOUT MY ABILITY TO	I FELT PROUD WHEN
SOMETHING I DID FOR SOMEONE ELSE	I TRIED
SOMETHING I DID FOR MYSELF	I FELT GOOD ABOUT MYSELF WHEN
I TOOK CARE OF MYSELF	I LEARNED
I ACCOMPLISHED	I CHALLENGED MYSELF TO

MONDAY:

TUESDAY:

WEDNESDAY:

THURSDAY:

FRIDAY:

SATURDAY:

SUNDAY:

SELF LOVE GROCERY LIST

As you create your grocery list for the week try to incorporate at least one food into each of the following categories to ensure you are taking care of your whole body, mind, and spirit. Plan your trips to the grocery store not just for food to eat but rather food that nourishes you. Under Meal Challenge-- think of a recipe you have been wanting to try, a food you want to cut out or add in to your diet. Do this weekly to see a drastic change in your overall health.

BRAIN FOOD	GUT HEALTH
SKIN AND HAIR CARE	**SLEEP**
HEALTHY INDULGENCES	**HEALTHY MUNCHIES**
HOUSEHOLD	**MEAL CHALLENGE**

YOUR WEEKLY WHY

Use this space to learn, grow and powerfully understand your thoughts and decision-making processes. Do this anytime you need clarity. Write it on a napkin, a back of an envelope, a journal, or anywhere you can write down and work through your thoughts.

The formula is simple.

Think of something during the week that excited you, upset you, stressed you out, made you inexplicably happy, or devastatingly sad. This could be an event, a choice, or even a conversation.

Then ask yourself WHY three times.

Seek solitude.

Until you are comfortable being alone you will not know if you are choosing someone out of love or loneliness.

Practice being alone.

Take yourself out to a meal without a guest or a phone.

Walk in nature alone (safely). Find a trail that opens you heart and eyes to the beauty of your surroundings.

Join a class where you know no one.

Go to an event alone.

Take yourself out on a proper date. Get dressed up. Woo yourself.

MY NEEDS THIS WEEK

Brainstorm your needs this week. Prioritize by number and add to your weekly calendar.

PERSONAL NEEDS:

PROFESSIONAL NEEDS:

SPIRITUAL NEEDS:

PHYSICAL NEEDS

EMOTIONAL NEEDS

PSYCHOLOGICAL NEEDS

IM POSSIBLE SELF WEEKLY SELF CARE PLAN

	MONDAY	TUESDAY	WEDNESDAY	THURSDAY	FRIDAY
PERSONAL					
PROFESSIONAL					
SPIRITUAL					
EMOTIONAL					
PHYSICAL					
PHYSICAL					

Reminders are personal mantras to be used in times of stress, decision-making, or in moments of gratitude and joy. Write your reminder for the week.

Support: Who or what will support you this week in your Self-Care goals.

REMINDERS	SUPPORT

WEEKEND SELF CARE PLAN

PERSONAL	
PROFESSIONAL	
SPIRITUAL	
EMOTIONAL	
PHYSICAL	
PSYCHOLOGICAL	

WEEKLY SELF ESTEEM CHECK IN

Choose 1 of the following prompts to respond to for each day of the week

SOMETHING I DID THAT MADE ME HAPPY	I FELT PROUD WHEN
SOMETHING I DID FOR SOMEONE ELSE	I TRIED
SOMETHING I POSITIVE I NOTICED	I FELT GOOD ABOUT MYSELF WHEN
I HAD A GOOD EXPERIENCE WITH	I LEARNED
I ACCOMPLISHED	I CHALLENGED MYSELF TO

MONDAY:

TUESDAY:

WEDNESDAY:

THURSDAY:

FRIDAY:

SATURDAY:

SUNDAY:

SELF LOVE GROCERY LIST

As you create your grocery list for the week try to incorporate at least one food into each of the following categories to ensure you are taking care of your whole body, mind, and spirit. Plan your trips to the grocery store not just for food to eat but rather food that nourishes you. Under Meal Challenge-- think of a recipe you have been wanting to try, a food you want to cut out or add in to your diet. Do this weekly to see a drastic change in your overall health.

BRAIN FOOD	GUT HEALTH
SKIN AND HAIR CARE	SLEEP
HEALTHY INDULGENCES	HEALTHY MUNCHIES
HOUSEHOLD	MEAL CHALLENGE

<u>YOUR WEEKLY WHY</u>

Use this space to learn, grow and powerfully understand your thoughts and decision-making processes. Do this anytime you need clarity. Write it on a napkin, a back of an envelope, a journal, or anywhere you can write down and work through your thoughts.

The formula is simple.

Think of something during the week that excited you, upset you, stressed you out, made you inexplicably happy, or devastatingly sad. This could be an event, a choice, or even a conversation.

Then ask yourself WHY three times.

MY NEEDS THIS WEEK

Brainstorm your needs this week. Prioritize by number and add to your weekly calendar.

PERSONAL NEEDS:

PROFESSIONAL NEEDS:

SPIRITUAL NEEDS:

PHYSICAL NEEDS

EMOTIONAL NEEDS

PSYCHOLOGICAL NEEDS

IM POSSIBLE SELF WEEKLY SELF CARE PLAN

	MONDAY	TUESDAY	WEDNESDAY	THURSDAY	FRIDAY
PERSONAL					
PROFESSIONAL					
SPIRITUAL					
EMOTIONAL					
PHYSICAL					
PHYSICAL					

Reminders are personal mantras to be used in times of stress, decision-making, or in moments of gratitude and joy. Write your reminder for the week.

Support: Who or what will support you this week in your Self-Care goals.

REMINDERS	SUPPORT

Your soul will always speak to you. Your gut will always whisper your truth back to you. If you pay attention, if you choose to honor your inner voice and respect your inner self, that faint whisper will become a roar. Everything you need will become clear. In moments of silence and in moments of commotion, your purpose, your truth and your most authentic self will be ever present.

We often refer to the whispers as signs. We notice patterns, we find ourselves gravitating back to the same old dreams, to the same narrative that tells us we are meant for a life of peace, joy, and fulfillment. We call them nudges, little winks from God.

Call them whatever you wish, but notice them, honor them and thank them for their presence. Let your inner voice be heard. ROAR.

What whispers have you been hearing from deep inside? Are you ready for those whispers to become a roar? What can you do today to give your inner voice permission to be heard?

WEEKEND SELF CARE PLAN

PERSONAL

PROFESSIONAL

SPIRITUAL

EMOTIONAL

PHYSICAL

PSYCHOLOGICAL

WEEKLY SELF ESTEEM CHECK IN

Choose 1 of the following prompts to respond to for each day of the week

I MADE PROGRESS WITH	I FELT PROUD WHEN
SOMETHING I DID FOR SOMEONE ELSE	I TRIED
SOMETHING I ENJOYED	I FELT GOOD ABOUT MYSELF WHEN
I HAD A GOOD EXPERIENCE WITH	I OBSERVED ABOUT MYSELF (POSITIVE)
I ACCOMPLISHED	I CHALLENGED MYSELF TO

MONDAY:

TUESDAY:

WEDNESDAY:

THURSDAY:

FRIDAY:

SATURDAY:

SUNDAY:

SELF LOVE GROCERY LIST

As you create your grocery list for the week try to incorporate at least one food into each of the following categories to ensure you are taking care of your whole body, mind, and spirit. Plan your trips to the grocery store not just for food to eat but rather food that nourishes you. Under Meal Challenge-- think of a recipe you have been wanting to try, a food you want to cut out or add in to your diet. Do this weekly to see a drastic change in your overall health.

BRAIN FOOD	GUT HEALTH
SKIN AND HAIR CARE	SLEEP
HEALTHY INDULGENCES	HEALTHY MUNCHIES
HOUSEHOLD	MEAL CHALLENGE

YOUR WEEKLY WHY

Use this space to learn, grow and powerfully understand your thoughts and decision-making processes. Do this anytime you need clarity. Write it on a napkin, a back of an envelope, a journal, or anywhere you can write down and work through your thoughts.

The formula is simple.

Think of something during the week that excited you, upset you, stressed you out, made you inexplicably happy, or devastatingly sad. This could be an event, a choice, or even a conversation.

Then ask yourself WHY three times.

MY NEEDS THIS WEEK

Brainstorm your needs this week. Prioritize by number and add to your weekly calendar.

PERSONAL NEEDS:

PROFESSIONAL NEEDS:

SPIRITUAL NEEDS:

PHYSICAL NEEDS

EMOTIONAL NEEDS

PSYCHOLOGICAL NEEDS

IM POSSIBLE SELF WEEKLY SELF CARE PLAN

	MONDAY	TUESDAY	WEDNESDAY	THURSDAY	FRIDAY
PERSONAL					
PROFESSIONAL					
SPIRITUAL					
EMOTIONAL					
PHYSICAL					
PHYSICAL					

Reminders are personal mantras to be used in times of stress, decision-making, or in moments of gratitude and joy. Write your reminder for the week.

Support: Who or what will support you this week in your Self-Care goals.

REMINDERS	SUPPORT

WEEKEND SELF CARE PLAN

PERSONAL	
PROFESSIONAL	
SPIRITUAL	
EMOTIONAL	
PHYSICAL	
PSYCHOLOGICAL	

WEEKLY SELF ESTEEM CHECK IN

Choose 1 of the following prompts to respond to for each day of the week

SOMETHING I FELT CONFIDENT IN	I FELT PROUD WHEN
SOMETHING I DID FOR SOMEONE ELSE	A CHOICE I MADE FOR MYSELF WAS
SOMETHING I DID FOR MYSELF	I FELT GOOD ABOUT MYSELF WHEN
I HAD A GOOD EXPERIENCE WITH	I LEARNED
I ACCOMPLISHED	I CHALLENGED MYSELF TO

MONDAY:

TUESDAY:

WEDNESDAY:

THURSDAY:

FRIDAY:

SATURDAY:

SUNDAY:

SELF LOVE GROCERY LIST

As you create your grocery list for the week try to incorporate at least one food into each of the following categories to ensure you are taking care of your whole body, mind, and spirit. Plan your trips to the grocery store not just for food to eat but rather food that nourishes you. Under Meal Challenge-- think of a recipe you have been wanting to try, a food you want to cut out or add in to your diet. Do this weekly to see a drastic change in your overall health.

BRAIN FOOD	GUT HEALTH
SKIN AND HAIR CARE	SLEEP
HEALTHY INDULGENCES	HEALTHY MUNCHIES
HOUSEHOLD	MEAL CHALLENGE

YOUR WEEKLY WHY

Use this space to learn, grow and powerfully understand your thoughts and decision-making processes. Do this anytime you need clarity. Write it on a napkin, a back of an envelope, a journal, or anywhere you can write down and work through your thoughts.

The formula is simple.

Think of something during the week that excited you, upset you, stressed you out, made you inexplicably happy, or devastatingly sad. This could be an event, a choice, or even a conversation.

Then ask yourself WHY three times.

CHOICE MAKING FLOW CHART

PROBLEM:

SOLUTION OPTIONS

OPTION ONE	OPTION TWO	OPTION THREE

Positive Outcomes   Positive Outcomes   Positive Outcomes

Negative Outcomes   Negative Outcomes   Negative Outcomes

SOLUTION CHOSEN

_____

_____

_____

5 MINUTE REFLECTIONS

THE UN-DO LIST

What distracted me from my self-care and self-love goals this month?

What caused me stress?

What did I do that wasn't my responsibility and overwhelmed me?

What drained my energy?

What did I say to myself that was hurtful or unnecessary?

One habit that didn't serve me this month?

Automatic Thoughts

Our thoughts pilot how we feel about ourselves and the world we live in. Many times, we fall into a cycle of automatic thinking. Automatic thinking can be damaging and problematic because the thought might be irrational, self-defeating or even untrue. This worksheet will help you identify some of your automatic thoughts, the roots of those thoughts and how to challenge those thoughts.

EXAMPLE:

TRIGGER	AUTOMATIC THOUGHTS	NEW THOUGHTS
Notices someone succeeding on social media. They are traveling and living a luxurious lifestyle.	My life looks nothing like that. I must be failing. I could never make the money to do all of that. I am stuck.	Their life seems nice but think of all the things they can't do that I can. If they are always on planes and in hotels, they don't get to see their family as much or enjoy time with friends like I. do. I am not failing. I am just doing life differently than that and I like the things I get to do. I have great friends; a wonderful relationship and I am happy. I would like to travel more so I should make it a priority and save up some money and actually plan for it.

TRIGGER	AUTOMATIC THOUGHTS	NEW THOUGHTS

TIPS FOR SELF CARE

Professional:	Personal:	Spiritual:
Integrate play into your daily schedule. Our minds are always at work even when we are not directly focused on something. By taking time for play or fun (even just singing in car) you use other parts of your brain allowing for new ideas and solutions to emerge effortlessly.	**Establish a morning routine that makes you happy.** What is the one thing you can do each morning that is a positive activity and brings you joy?	**Cleanse your space.** Remove negative energy from your space. This can be removing old pictures, letters, albums...anything that brings you down.
Physical:	**Emotional:**	**Psychological:**
Avoid a carb hangover. Eating nutrient dense foods will ultimately give you more energy and you won't crash into a food coma...which only will make you lazy and want more comfort food...which will make you feel terrible...which starts the whole cycle over again.	**Take time to focus on a pleasurable memory.** Write down or speak out loud all the things about that memory that make you feel good.	**Move that belly!** Use your diaphragm to take deep breathes. As your breath relaxes your body it will also relax your mind.

"You are uniquely and beautifully created with a purpose no one else in this world has. When we truly understand this, there is no such thing as competition, only cheering one another on and bettering ourselves."

-Daphne DeLoren

MY NEEDS THIS WEEK

Brainstorm your needs this week. Prioritize by number and add to your weekly calendar.

PERSONAL NEEDS:

PROFESSIONAL NEEDS:

SPIRITUAL NEEDS:

PHYSICAL NEEDS

EMOTIONAL NEEDS

PSYCHOLOGICAL NEEDS

IM POSSIBLE SELF WEEKLY SELF CARE PLAN

	MONDAY	TUESDAY	WEDNESDAY	THURSDAY	FRIDAY
PERSONAL					
PROFESSIONAL					
SPIRITUAL					
EMOTIONAL					
PHYSICAL					
PHYSICAL					

Reminders are personal mantras to be used in times of stress, decision-making, or in moments of gratitude and joy. Write your reminder for the week.

Support: Who or what will support you this week in your Self-Care goals.

REMINDERS	SUPPORT

WEEKEND SELF CARE PLAN

PERSONAL

PROFESSIONAL

SPIRITUAL

EMOTIONAL

PHYSICAL

PSYCHOLOGICAL

WEEKLY SELF ESTEEM CHECK IN

Choose 1 of the following prompts to respond to for each day of the week

SOMETHING I DID WELL WAS	I FELT PROUD WHEN
SOMETHING I DID FOR SOMEONE ELSE	I USED PATIENCE WHEN
SOMETHING I DID FOR MYSELF	I FELT GOOD ABOUT MYSELF WHEN
I HAD A GOOD EXPERIENCE WITH	I USED KINDESS WHEN
A GOAL I SET WAS	I CHALLENGED MYSELF TO

MONDAY:

TUESDAY:

WEDNESDAY:

THURSDAY:

FRIDAY:

SATURDAY:

SUNDAY:

SELF LOVE GROCERY LIST

As you create your grocery list for the week try to incorporate at least one food into each of the following categories to ensure you are taking care of your whole body, mind, and spirit. Plan your trips to the grocery store not just for food to eat but rather food that nourishes you. Under Meal Challenge-- think of a recipe you have been wanting to try, a food you want to cut out or add in to your diet. Do this weekly to see a drastic change in your overall health.

BRAIN FOOD	GUT HEALTH
SKIN AND HAIR CARE	SLEEP
HEALTHY INDULGENCES	HEALTHY MUNCHIES
HOUSEHOLD	MEAL CHALLENGE

YOUR WEEKLY WHY

Use this space to learn, grow and powerfully understand your thoughts and decision-making processes. Do this anytime you need clarity. Write it on a napkin, a back of an envelope, a journal, or anywhere you can write down and work through your thoughts.

The formula is simple.

Think of something during the week that excited you, upset you, stressed you out, made you inexplicably happy, or devastatingly sad. This could be an event, a choice, or even a conversation.

Then ask yourself WHY three times.

MY NEEDS THIS WEEK

Brainstorm your needs this week. Prioritize by number and add to your weekly calendar.

PERSONAL NEEDS:

PROFESSIONAL NEEDS:

SPIRITUAL NEEDS:

PHYSICAL NEEDS

EMOTIONAL NEEDS

PSYCHOLOGICAL NEEDS

IM POSSIBLE SELF WEEKLY SELF CARE PLAN

	MONDAY	TUESDAY	WEDNESDAY	THURSDAY	FRIDAY
PERSONAL					
PROFESSIONAL					
SPIRITUAL					
EMOTIONAL					
PHYSICAL					
PHYSICAL					

Reminders are personal mantras to be used in times of stress, decision-making, or in moments of gratitude and joy. Write your reminder for the week.

Support: Who or what will support you this week in your Self-Care goals.

REMINDERS	SUPPORT

WEEKEND SELF CARE PLAN

PERSONAL

PROFESSIONAL

SPIRITUAL

EMOTIONAL

PHYSICAL

PSYCHOLOGICAL

WEEKLY SELF ESTEEM CHECK IN

Choose 1 of the following prompts to respond to for each day of the week

SOMETHING I DID FELT GOOD ABOUT	I FELT PROUD WHEN
SOMETHING I DID FOR SOMEONE ELSE	I REACHED OUT TO
SOMETHING I DID FOR MYSELF	I FELT GOOD ABOUT MYSELF WHEN
I MET	I LEARNED
I ACCOMPLISHED	I CHALLENGED MYSELF TO

MONDAY:

TUESDAY:

WEDNESDAY:

THURSDAY:

FRIDAY:

SATURDAY:

SUNDAY:

ORANGE SCRUB

Many times, the people that need our love the most ask for it in the most unloving ways.

Our body is no different.

Take care of your body or it will scream for your love.

Here is a simple recipe for a DIY body polish with the added benefit of increasing magnesium. Magnesium helps the body fight imbalances.

The orange adds a little zest to your morning. Think of it as sunshine in a jar.

Mint eases muscle pains. Why start your day achy?

Simply mix together Epsom salt, orange essential oil, and either fresh mint leaves or mint essential oils. Add a little coconut oil. Keep in a glass jar with a lid and use daily for an invigorating shower experience.

SELF LOVE GROCERY LIST

As you create your grocery list for the week try to incorporate at least one food into each of the following categories to ensure you are taking care of your whole body, mind, and spirit. Plan your trips to the grocery store not just for food to eat but rather food that nourishes you. Under Meal Challenge-- think of a recipe you have been wanting to try, a food you want to cut out or add in to your diet. Do this weekly to see a drastic change in your overall health.

BRAIN FOOD	GUT HEALTH
SKIN AND HAIR CARE	SLEEP
HEALTHY INDULGENCES	HEALTHY MUNCHIES
HOUSEHOLD	MEAL CHALLENGE

YOUR WEEKLY WHY

Use this space to learn, grow and powerfully understand your thoughts and decision-making processes. Do this anytime you need clarity. Write it on a napkin, a back of an envelope, a journal, or anywhere you can write down and work through your thoughts.

The formula is simple.

Think of something during the week that excited you, upset you, stressed you out, made you inexplicably happy, or devastatingly sad. This could be an event, a choice, or even a conversation.

Then ask yourself WHY three times.

MY NEEDS THIS WEEK

Brainstorm your needs this week. Prioritize by number and add to your weekly calendar.

PERSONAL NEEDS:

PROFESSIONAL NEEDS:

SPIRITUAL NEEDS:

PHYSICAL NEEDS

EMOTIONAL NEEDS

PSYCHOLOGICAL NEEDS

IM POSSIBLE SELF WEEKLY SELF CARE PLAN

	MONDAY	TUESDAY	WEDNESDAY	THURSDAY	FRIDAY
PERSONAL					
PROFESSIONAL					
SPIRITUAL					
EMOTIONAL					
PHYSICAL					
PHYSICAL					

Reminders are personal mantras to be used in times of stress, decision-making, or in moments of gratitude and joy. Write your reminder for the week.

Support: Who or what will support you this week in your Self-Care goals.

REMINDERS	SUPPORT

WEEKEND SELF CARE PLAN

PERSONAL	
PROFESSIONAL	
SPIRITUAL	
EMOTIONAL	
PHYSICAL	
PSYCHOLOGICAL	

WEEKLY SELF ESTEEM CHECK IN

Choose 1 of the following prompts to respond to for each day of the week

SOMETHING I DID WELL WAS	I FELT PROUD WHEN
SOMETHING I DID FOR SOMEONE ELSE	I SUCCEEDED AT
SOMETHING THAT INSPIRED ME	I FELT GOOD ABOUT MYSELF WHEN
I HAD A GOOD EXPERIENCE WITH	I CONTRIBUTED TO
I ACCOMPLISHED	I CHALLENGED MYSELF TO

MONDAY:

TUESDAY:

WEDNESDAY:

THURSDAY:

FRIDAY:

SATURDAY:

SUNDAY:

SELF LOVE GROCERY LIST

As you create your grocery list for the week try to incorporate at least one food into each of the following categories to ensure you are taking care of your whole body, mind, and spirit. Plan your trips to the grocery store not just for food to eat but rather food that nourishes you. Under Meal Challenge-- think of a recipe you have been wanting to try, a food you want to cut out or add in to your diet. Do this weekly to see a drastic change in your overall health.

BRAIN FOOD	GUT HEALTH
SKIN AND HAIR CARE	**SLEEP**
HEALTHY INDULGENCES	**HEALTHY MUNCHIES**
HOUSEHOLD	**MEAL CHALLENGE**

YOUR WEEKLY WHY

Use this space to learn, grow and powerfully understand your thoughts and decision-making processes. Do this anytime you need clarity. Write it on a napkin, a back of an envelope, a journal, or anywhere you can write down and work through your thoughts.

The formula is simple.

Think of something during the week that excited you, upset you, stressed you out, made you inexplicably happy, or devastatingly sad. This could be an event, a choice, or even a conversation.

Then ask yourself WHY three times.

MY NEEDS THIS WEEK

Brainstorm your needs this week. Prioritize by number and add to your weekly calendar.

PERSONAL NEEDS:

PROFESSIONAL NEEDS:

SPIRITUAL NEEDS:

PHYSICAL NEEDS

EMOTIONAL NEEDS

PSYCHOLOGICAL NEEDS

IM POSSIBLE SELF WEEKLY SELF CARE PLAN

	MONDAY	TUESDAY	WEDNESDAY	THURSDAY	FRIDAY
PERSONAL					
PROFESSIONAL					
SPIRITUAL					
EMOTIONAL					
PHYSICAL					
PHYSICAL					

Reminders are personal mantras to be used in times of stress, decision-making, or in moments of gratitude and joy. Write your reminder for the week.

Support: Who or what will support you this week in your Self-Care goals.

REMINDERS	SUPPORT

WEEKEND SELF CARE PLAN

PERSONAL	
PROFESSIONAL	
SPIRITUAL	
EMOTIONAL	
PHYSICAL	
PSYCHOLOGICAL	

<u>WEEKLY SELF ESTEEM CHECK IN</u>

Choose 1 of the following prompts to respond to for each day of the week

SOMETHING I DID THAT MADE ME HAPPY	I FELT PROUD WHEN
SOMETHING I DID FOR SOMEONE ELSE	I TRIED
SOMETHING I DID FOR MYSELF	I FELT GOOD ABOUT MYSELF WHEN
I ENJOYED	I LEARNED
I ACCOMPLISHED	I SET THE GOAL OF

MONDAY:

TUESDAY:

WEDNESDAY:

THURSDAY:

FRIDAY:

SATURDAY:

SUNDAY:

SELF LOVE GROCERY LIST

As you create your grocery list for the week try to incorporate at least one food into each of the following categories to ensure you are taking care of your whole body, mind, and spirit. Plan your trips to the grocery store not just for food to eat but rather food that nourishes you. Under Meal Challenge-- think of a recipe you have been wanting to try, a food you want to cut out or add in to your diet. Do this weekly to see a drastic change in your overall health.

BRAIN FOOD	GUT HEALTH
SKIN AND HAIR CARE	**SLEEP**
HEALTHY INDULGENCES	**HEALTHY MUNCHIES**
HOUSEHOLD	**MEAL CHALLENGE**

YOUR WEEKLY WHY

Use this space to learn, grow and powerfully understand your thoughts and decision-making processes. Do this anytime you need clarity. Write it on a napkin, a back of an envelope, a journal, or anywhere you can write down and work through your thoughts.

The formula is simple.

Think of something during the week that excited you, upset you, stressed you out, made you inexplicably happy, or devastatingly sad. This could be an event, a choice, or even a conversation.

Then ask yourself WHY three times.

LIBERATION LETTER

Use this template to write a letter to someone or something you must release in order to move forward. This letter is meant for you to acknowledge the people, habits or activities that are no longer serving you. Use this template once a month to allow for optimal growth. Use this page or ideally a separate sheet of paper to allow for thoughtful responses.

Dear,

I am choosing to say goodbye because

You should know saying goodbye makes me feel

I would like to thank you for showing me

I have learned

I now know that

I am ready to

When I say goodbye to you I will no longer

Sincerely,

HELLO LETTER

Now that you have said goodbye to someone or something that has been holding you back from taking care of yourself and living abundantly, you must check in with yourself. This step is crucial as it will promote healing, create a plan to truly move forward and aid in closure. Use template once a month to allow for optimal growth. Use this page or ideally a separate sheet of paper to allow for thoughtful responses.

Dear,

I just said goodbye to

Saying goodbye to makes me feel

but I know it is for the best. Some of the reasons I know this is for the best are because

Moving forward will be hard. That is ok. Please allow yourself time to feel

Some things you can do when you feel upset about closing this chapter are

Some people you can talk to are

There will be ups and downs, good days and bad days. That is part of difficult change, and it is normal and OK. On the really hard days a reminder you can use is

On the really great days a reminder you can use is

Here are three things I feel confident I can do to move forward and say goodbye

1.

2.

3.

Lastly, thank you for acknowledging it was time to let go. Thank you for honoring your health and your spirit. You deserve the best life has to offer and I am proud of you for putting yourself first.

Love always,

REGULATORS!

Emotions are complicated, so let's work to uncomplicate them. Sometimes our emotions are so intense they cloud our thinking and our judgement. This simple activity will help you sort through your emotions and transform your thinking around the emotion, making it more manageable.

	Example	You Try!
Identify	Anxiety about applying for a new job and starting career path over.	
Resulting action	Avoid looking at job postings and revising resume. Stay stuck in the job longer and be miserable every day.	
Flip it and reverse it	Push yourself to think of yourself as jobs interviewing for you. You are not starting over but rather they will be adding opportunity to your life in some way with what they offer. You will be brining your experience and expertise to the job and they are there to support you as your level up your career.	
New action	Look for jobs that fit your skill set and get excited about the opportunity to reach a higher potential.	

5 MINUTE REFLECTION

Gratitude

One sensation you were grateful this month?

One experience you were grateful for this month

One person you were grateful for this month:

Why were you grateful for that person?

What did you learn from this person about kindness?

How can you pay what you learned forward?

What qualities do you admire in this person?

Do you believe you possess some of the same qualities?

List 4 things that happened this month that you are grateful for

Write out what is going really well in your life right now

TIPS FOR SELF CARE

Professional:	Personal:	Spiritual:
Allow yourself to be uncreative. Sometimes self-care means taking a break from everything that asks you perform, produce or be "on."	**Take yourself out on a date.** No phone, no tablet or computer. Just you and YOU. Experience your surroundings, take a few deep breaths, LISTEN to yourself and ENJOY your own company.	Meditate
Physical:	**Emotional:**	**Psychological:**
Get more sleep. Keep the tip of your tongue resting lightly behind the front upper teeth throughout this whole exercise. Exhale from lungs Inhale through the nose for 4 counts Exhale through mouth to the count of 8, making an audible WHOOOSH. Repeat this cycle 4 times to fall fast asleep.	CRY.	**Write it out.** Whether you use a journal, or back of a bill, write it out. Grammar doesn't matter. Just release the words that are hurting you.

"Nothing lasts forever and that goes for both the good and the bad. If you are going through a difficult time, you can know with certainty it will pass. And if you are experiencing something exceptional, well, you'd better be present. Soak up the good while you are in it because more of life's moments, experiences and events are just around the bend. In my experience, the best indicator of your current state of being is how you navigate change. That is where we grow into the humans you hope to be."

-Jennifer Newman

<u>MY NEEDS THIS WEEK</u>

Brainstorm your needs this week. Prioritize by number and add to your weekly calendar.

PERSONAL NEEDS:

PROFESSIONAL NEEDS:

SPIRITUAL NEEDS:

PHYSICAL NEEDS

EMOTIONAL NEEDS

PSYCHOLOGICAL NEEDS

IM POSSIBLE SELF WEEKLY SELF CARE PLAN

	MONDAY	TUESDAY	WEDNESDAY	THURSDAY	FRIDAY
PERSONAL					
PROFESSIONAL					
SPIRITUAL					
EMOTIONAL					
PHYSICAL					
PHYSICAL					

Reminders are personal mantras to be used in times of stress, decision-making, or in moments of gratitude and joy. Write your reminder for the week.

Support: Who or what will support you this week in your Self-Care goals.

REMINDERS	SUPPORT

WEEKEND SELF CARE PLAN

PERSONAL	
PROFESSIONAL	
SPIRITUAL	
EMOTIONAL	
PHYSICAL	
PSYCHOLOGICAL	

WEEKLY SELF ESTEEM CHECK IN

Choose 2 of the following prompts to respond to for each day of the week

SOMETHING I FOCUSED ON	I FELT PROUD WHEN
SOMETHING I DID FOR SOMEONE ELSE	I FELT LOVED WHEN
SOMETHING I DID FOR MYSELF	I FELT GOOD ABOUT MYSELF WHEN
I MADE PROGRESS ON	I LEARNED
I ACCOMPLISHED	I CHALLENGED MYSELF TO

MONDAY:

TUESDAY:

WEDNESDAY:

THURSDAY:

FRIDAY:

SATURDAY:

SUNDAY:

SELF LOVE GROCERY LIST

As you create your grocery list for the week try to incorporate at least one food into each of the following categories to ensure you are taking care of your whole body, mind, and spirit. Plan your trips to the grocery store not just for food to eat but rather food that nourishes you. Under Meal Challenge-- think of a recipe you have been wanting to try, a food you want to cut out or add in to your diet. Do this weekly to see a drastic change in your overall health.

BRAIN FOOD	GUT HEALTH
SKIN AND HAIR CARE	SLEEP
HEALTHY INDULGENCES	HEALTHY MUNCHIES
HOUSEHOLD	MEAL CHALLENGE

YOUR WEEKLY WHY

Use this space to learn, grow and powerfully understand your thoughts and decision-making processes. Do this anytime you need clarity. Write it on a napkin, a back of an envelope, a journal, or anywhere you can write down and work through your thoughts.

The formula is simple.

Think of something during the week that excited you, upset you, stressed you out, made you inexplicably happy, or devastatingly sad. This could be an event, a choice, or even a conversation.

Then ask yourself WHY three times.

What do I enjoy doing most when I am alone? What does this tell me about myself? What does this tell me about my needs?

Example: I love when I have a night to myself to watch episodes of Sex and The City. I take a long shower, pick up a monster size burrito and I eat it in bed. I like to fall asleep watching the show.

This tells me I enjoy the solitude of indulging in guilty pleasure sometimes. I like having the outlet to watch other people, even fictional, go through and learn through the same things I have. That show reminds me of adventures with friends. I find I always want to reach out and connect after I watch it. Maybe I need to make more time for old friendships. Check in more often. I think I may be needing those connections more than I thought.

I love burritos and it is pretty unsightly the way I eat it in bed. But I love it because I am free of judgement there. I think I need to look at my environment and notice how often I feel judged or unable to express my true self.

MY NEEDS THIS WEEK

Brainstorm your needs this week. Prioritize by number and add to your weekly calendar.

PERSONAL NEEDS:

PROFESSIONAL NEEDS:

SPIRITUAL NEEDS:

PHYSICAL NEEDS

EMOTIONAL NEEDS

PSYCHOLOGICAL NEEDS

IM POSSIBLE SELF WEEKLY SELF CARE PLAN

	MONDAY	TUESDAY	WEDNESDAY	THURSDAY	FRIDAY
PERSONAL					
PROFESSIONAL					
SPIRITUAL					
EMOTIONAL					
PHYSICAL					
PHYSICAL					

Reminders are personal mantras to be used in times of stress, decision-making, or in moments of gratitude and joy. Write your reminder for the week.

Support: Who or what will support you this week in your Self-Care goals.

REMINDERS	SUPPORT

WEEKEND SELF CARE PLAN

PERSONAL	
PROFESSIONAL	
SPIRITUAL	
EMOTIONAL	
PHYSICAL	
PSYCHOLOGICAL	

WEEKLY SELF ESTEEM CHECK IN

Choose 3 of the following prompts to respond to for each day of the week

SOMETHING I DID WELL WAS	I FELT PROUD WHEN
SOMETHING I DID FOR SOMEONE ELSE	I TRIED
SOMETHING I DID FOR MYSELF	I FELT GOOD ABOUT MYSELF WHEN
I HAD A GOOD EXPERIENCE WITH	I LEARNED
I ACCOMPLISHED	I CHALLENGED MYSELF TO

MONDAY:

TUESDAY:

WEDNESDAY:

THURSDAY:

FRIDAY:

SATURDAY:

SUNDAY:

SELF LOVE GROCERY LIST

As you create your grocery list for the week try to incorporate at least one food into each of the following categories to ensure you are taking care of your whole body, mind, and spirit. Plan your trips to the grocery store not just for food to eat but rather food that nourishes you. Under Meal Challenge-- think of a recipe you have been wanting to try, a food you want to cut out or add in to your diet. Do this weekly to see a drastic change in your overall health.

BRAIN FOOD	GUT HEALTH
SKIN AND HAIR CARE	SLEEP
HEALTHY INDULGENCES	HEALTHY MUNCHIES
HOUSEHOLD	MEAL CHALLENGE

YOUR WEEKLY WHY

Use this space to learn, grow and powerfully understand your thoughts and decision-making processes. Do this anytime you need clarity. Write it on a napkin, a back of an envelope, a journal, or anywhere you can write down and work through your thoughts.

The formula is simple.

Think of something during the week that excited you, upset you, stressed you out, made you inexplicably happy, or devastatingly sad. This could be an event, a choice, or even a conversation.

Then ask yourself WHY three times.

MY NEEDS THIS WEEK

Brainstorm your needs this week. Prioritize by number and add to your weekly calendar.

PERSONAL NEEDS:

PROFESSIONAL NEEDS:

SPIRITUAL NEEDS:

PHYSICAL NEEDS

EMOTIONAL NEEDS

PSYCHOLOGICAL NEEDS

IM POSSIBLE SELF WEEKLY SELF CARE PLAN

	MONDAY	TUESDAY	WEDNESDAY	THURSDAY	FRIDAY
PERSONAL					
PROFESSIONAL					
SPIRITUAL					
EMOTIONAL					
PHYSICAL					
PHYSICAL					

Reminders are personal mantras to be used in times of stress, decision-making, or in moments of gratitude and joy. Write your reminder for the week.

Support: Who or what will support you this week in your Self-Care goals.

REMINDERS	SUPPORT

WEEKEND SELF CARE PLAN

PERSONAL	
PROFESSIONAL	
SPIRITUAL	
EMOTIONAL	
PHYSICAL	
PSYCHOLOGICAL	

The struggle is real...and that is OK

So, you are struggling. Struggling does not make you unlovable, unworthy or a burden. Struggling does not make you undeserving of kindness or care. It doesn't mean that you are too much, or too sensitive or even too needy.

It means you are a human.

In each of our lives we will go through a season (sometimes several seasons) of struggle. There will be times you will fall apart. You will do and say things completely out of character.

During these times you may be difficult to be around. That is OK. No one is easy to be around 100% of the time. You may be unpleasant, you may be drama, you may make it really difficult to love you.

But those things are just the sum of the struggle you are experiencing; they are not the sum of who you are.

Struggle does not discount your worth.

Give yourself permission to go through the hard times. To be a pain. To be difficult and less than perfect. Life is messy. People are messy. Love is fucking messy.

You are human. You are worthy.

WEEKLY SELF ESTEEM CHECK IN

Choose 1 of the following prompts to respond to for each day of the week

SOMETHING I DID WELL WAS	I FELT PROUD WHEN
SOMETHING I DID FOR SOMEONE ELSE	I FELT CONNECTED TO
SOMETHING I DID FOR MYSELF	I FELT GOOD ABOUT MYSELF WHEN
I FAILED AT....BUT I FELT GOOD TRYING	I LEARNED
I SPENT QUALITY TIME WITH	I CHALLENGED MYSELF TO

MONDAY:

TUESDAY:

WEDNESDAY:

THURSDAY:

FRIDAY:

SATURDAY:

SUNDAY:

SELF LOVE GROCERY LIST

As you create your grocery list for the week try to incorporate at least one food into each of the following categories to ensure you are taking care of your whole body, mind, and spirit. Plan your trips to the grocery store not just for food to eat but rather food that nourishes you. Under Meal Challenge-- think of a recipe you have been wanting to try, a food you want to cut out or add in to your diet. Do this weekly to see a drastic change in your overall health.

BRAIN FOOD	GUT HEALTH
SKIN AND HAIR CARE	SLEEP
HEALTHY INDULGENCES	HEALTHY MUNCHIES
HOUSEHOLD	MEAL CHALLENGE

YOUR WEEKLY WHY

Use this space to learn, grow and powerfully understand your thoughts and decision-making processes. Do this anytime you need clarity. Write it on a napkin, a back of an envelope, a journal, or anywhere you can write down and work through your thoughts.

The formula is simple.

Think of something during the week that excited you, upset you, stressed you out, made you inexplicably happy, or devastatingly sad. This could be an event, a choice, or even a conversation.

Then ask yourself WHY three times.

MY NEEDS THIS WEEK

Brainstorm your needs this week. Prioritize by number and add to your weekly calendar.

PERSONAL NEEDS:

PROFESSIONAL NEEDS:

SPIRITUAL NEEDS:

PHYSICAL NEEDS

EMOTIONAL NEEDS

PSYCHOLOGICAL NEEDS

IM POSSIBLE SELF WEEKLY SELF CARE PLAN

	MONDAY	TUESDAY	WEDNESDAY	THURSDAY	FRIDAY
PERSONAL					
PROFESSIONAL					
SPIRITUAL					
EMOTIONAL					
PHYSICAL					
PHYSICAL					

Reminders are personal mantras to be used in times of stress, decision-making, or in moments of gratitude and joy. Write your reminder for the week.

Support: Who or what will support you this week in your Self-Care goals.

REMINDERS	SUPPORT

WEEKEND SELF CARE PLAN

PERSONAL	
PROFESSIONAL	
SPIRITUAL	
EMOTIONAL	
PHYSICAL	
PSYCHOLOGICAL	

WEEKLY SELF ESTEEM CHECK IN

Choose 1 of the following prompts to respond to for each day of the week

SOMETHING I DID WELL WAS	I FELT PROUD WHEN
SOMETHING I DID FOR SOMEONE ELSE	A COMPLIMENT I RECEIVED WAS
SOMETHING I DID FOR MYSELF	I FELT GOOD ABOUT MYSELF WHEN
I FELT LOVED BY	I EXPLORED
I ACCOMPLISHED	I CHALLENGED MYSELF TO

MONDAY:

TUESDAY:

WEDNESDAY:

THURSDAY:

FRIDAY:

SATURDAY:

SUNDAY:

SELF LOVE GROCERY LIST

As you create your grocery list for the week try to incorporate at least one food into each of the following categories to ensure you are taking care of your whole body, mind, and spirit. Plan your trips to the grocery store not just for food to eat but rather food that nourishes you. Under Meal Challenge-- think of a recipe you have been wanting to try, a food you want to cut out or add in to your diet. Do this weekly to see a drastic change in your overall health.

BRAIN FOOD	GUT HEALTH
SKIN AND HAIR CARE	**SLEEP**
HEALTHY INDULGENCES	**HEALTHY MUNCHIES**
HOUSEHOLD	**MEAL CHALLENGE**

YOUR WEEKLY WHY

Use this space to learn, grow and powerfully understand your thoughts and decision-making processes. Do this anytime you need clarity. Write it on a napkin, a back of an envelope, a journal, or anywhere you can write down and work through your thoughts.

The formula is simple.

Think of something during the week that excited you, upset you, stressed you out, made you inexplicably happy, or devastatingly sad. This could be an event, a choice, or even a conversation.

Then ask yourself WHY three times.

5 Minute Reflection

Habits

What habit would you like to break next month and why? How would your happiness improve without this habit?

What habit would you like to start the next month? How would your happiness improve?

Choose a date next month to begin breaking an unfulfilling habit or starting an empowering habit. Look at your calendar and choose a date that will work best for your schedule and focus. The idea is to set yourself up for success. Are Monday's always crazy? Choose a Wednesday start date. Too many events the first half of the month to focus? Choose a date in the second half of the month. Look at what you are choosing to start or stop and aim for a day that will nurture your goal not work against it.

LIBERATION LETTER

Use this template to write a letter to someone or something you must release in order to move forward. This letter is meant for you to acknowledge the people, habits or activities that are no longer serving you. Use this template once a month to allow for optimal growth. Use this page or ideally a separate sheet of paper to allow for thoughtful responses.

Dear,

I am choosing to say goodbye because

You should know saying goodbye makes me feel

You have taught me

I learned

I now understand

When I say goodbye to you I will no longer

You will know I have said goodbye because

Sincerely,

HELLO LETTER

Now that you have said goodbye to someone or something that has been holding you back from taking care of yourself and living abundantly, you must check in with yourself. This step is crucial as it will promote healing, create a plan to truly move forward and aid in closure. Use template once a month to allow for optimal growth. Use this page or ideally a separate sheet of paper to allow for thoughtful responses.

Dear,

I just said goodbye to

Saying goodbye to makes me feel

but I know it is for the best. Some of the reasons I know this is for the best are because

Moving forward will be hard. That is ok. Please allow yourself time to feel

Some things you can do when you feel upset about closing this chapter are

Some people you can talk to are

There will be ups and downs, good days and bad days. That is part of difficult change, and it is normal and OK. On the really hard days a reminder you can use is

On the really great days a reminder you can use is

Here are three things I feel confident I can do to move forward and say goodbye

1.

2.

3.

Lastly, thank you for acknowledging it was time to let go. Thank you for honoring your health and your spirit. You deserve the best life has to offer and I am proud of you for putting yourself first.

Love always,

COPING MECHANISMS

Think of something that is causing stress to be present in your life. Write it down. There may be many things or just one. Write it all down. Then respond to the prompts below in reference to your current stressor.

REFRAME:

Can you reframe this stress to look at through the perspective of "What is this teaching me?" or "What opportunities may come from this?" Write down a reframed perspective using those prompts to address your current stressor.

COPING:

Identify your coping mechanisms. Identify what doesn't work in the LONG RUN. Many short-term solutions are unhealthy but yield "quick fixes." **Understand your coping mechanisms and make sure they are not actually adding to your stress.** What coping mechanisms are you currently using? Are those methods helping or harming?

GET IN THE ZONE

Let's take a look at the bubble we call the "comfort zone." Are there ways to expand that zone that could benefit you?

What people, places and things are inside of my comfort zone?

What sits just outside of my comfort zone but intriguing to me?

Is there something outside of my comfort zone I have pushed myself to do and felt good about afterwards? Could I do it again?

What small steps (steps that feel safe) I could take to expand my comfort zone to allow for a new opportunity and self-exploration?

Standing behind every successful woman is **herself.**

Cheering on every happy woman is **herself.**

Unabashedly rooting for every peaceful woman is **herself.**

How can you advocate for yourself today?

TIPS FOR SELF CARE

Professional:	Personal:	Spiritual:
Make your bed. It might seem too simple to be effective but starting your day with an accomplishment is a great way to shift your morning mood. This 2-minute routine can set you up for the rest of your day!	**Speak out LOUD** Find a place you won't look crazy (not the grocery store or standing in line at bank) and speak to yourself OUT LOUD. Hearing your thoughts outside of the static of your mind will help you find immense clarity and form a relationship with your inner voice resulting in better choices and overall happiness.	**Yoga.** Even if Yoga isn't your thing, search for a class that is more your vibe. Some studios offer hip hop yoga, others offer yoga with sound baths. Find what speaks to you.
Physical:	**Emotional:**	**Psychological:**
Get moving. Even if it is a dance while folding laundry, or some squats emptying the dishwasher—move your body!	**Laugh.** Who or what makes you laugh the most? Go spend time with that person or doing that thing. Laughter is essential.	**My Therapist says...** Try therapy. If you are really stuck and you know in your gut you need some extra help, reach out to a therapist! The most loving thing you can do for yourself is to say "I see you suffering and I will commit to helping you."

"One of the first things we do as a baby is laugh. As we get older life gets harder and laughter becomes less natural but more needed. I hope humans never stop making each other laugh, sharing jokes or even just a smile. What helps us get through this impossible difficult, crazy life full of hardships and pain is the abundant healing power in humor."

-Laura Thompson

MY NEEDS THIS WEEK

Brainstorm your needs this week. Prioritize by number and add to your weekly calendar.

PERSONAL NEEDS:

PROFESSIONAL NEEDS:

SPIRITUAL NEEDS:

PHYSICAL NEEDS

EMOTIONAL NEEDS

PSYCHOLOGICAL NEEDS

IM POSSIBLE SELF WEEKLY SELF CARE PLAN

	MONDAY	TUESDAY	WEDNESDAY	THURSDAY	FRIDAY
PERSONAL					
PROFESSIONAL					
SPIRITUAL					
EMOTIONAL					
PHYSICAL					
PHYSICAL					

Reminders are personal mantras to be used in times of stress, decision-making, or in moments of gratitude and joy. Write your reminder for the week.

Support: Who or what will support you this week in your Self-Care goals.

REMINDERS	SUPPORT

WEEKEND SELF CARE PLAN

PERSONAL	
PROFESSIONAL	
SPIRITUAL	
EMOTIONAL	
PHYSICAL	
PSYCHOLOGICAL	

<u>WEEKLY SELF ESTEEM CHECK IN</u>

Choose 2 of the following prompts to respond to for each day of the week

I WAS KIND TO	I FELT PROUD WHEN
SOMETHING I DID FOR SOMEONE ELSE	I SPOKE UP WHEN
SOMETHING I DID FOR MYSELF	I FELT GOOD ABOUT MYSELF WHEN
I ADVOCATED FOR MYSELF WHEN	I LEARNED
I ACCOMPLISHED	I CHALLENGED MYSELF TO

MONDAY:

TUESDAY:

WEDNESDAY:

THURSDAY:

FRIDAY:

SATURDAY:

SUNDAY:

SELF LOVE GROCERY LIST

As you create your grocery list for the week try to incorporate at least one food into each of the following categories to ensure you are taking care of your whole body, mind, and spirit. Plan your trips to the grocery store not just for food to eat but rather food that nourishes you. Under Meal Challenge-- think of a recipe you have been wanting to try, a food you want to cut out or add in to your diet. Do this weekly to see a drastic change in your overall health.

BRAIN FOOD	GUT HEALTH
SKIN AND HAIR CARE	SLEEP
HEALTHY INDULGENCES	HEALTHY MUNCHIES
HOUSEHOLD	MEAL CHALLENGE

YOUR WEEKLY WHY

Use this space to learn, grow and powerfully understand your thoughts and decision-making processes. Do this anytime you need clarity. Write it on a napkin, a back of an envelope, a journal, or anywhere you can write down and work through your thoughts.

The formula is simple.

Think of something during the week that excited you, upset you, stressed you out, made you inexplicably happy, or devastatingly sad. This could be an event, a choice, or even a conversation.

Then ask yourself WHY three times.

MY NEEDS THIS WEEK

Brainstorm your needs this week. Prioritize by number and add to your weekly calendar.

PERSONAL NEEDS:

PROFESSIONAL NEEDS:

SPIRITUAL NEEDS:

PHYSICAL NEEDS

EMOTIONAL NEEDS

PSYCHOLOGICAL NEEDS

It is not the future you fear; it is repeating the past that terrifies you.

What are you afraid of repeating? What steps can you take to ensure you do not repeat that element of your past?

Write it down. Create a verbal reminder to use when confronted with situations that beckon you to repeat a mistake, pattern or unhealthy choice.

IM POSSIBLE SELF WEEKLY SELF CARE PLAN

	MONDAY	TUESDAY	WEDNESDAY	THURSDAY	FRIDAY
PERSONAL					
PROFESSIONAL					
SPIRITUAL					
EMOTIONAL					
PHYSICAL					
PHYSICAL					

Reminders are personal mantras to be used in times of stress, decision-making, or in moments of gratitude and joy. Write your reminder for the week.

Support: Who or what will support you this week in your Self-Care goals.

REMINDERS	SUPPORT

WEEKEND SELF CARE PLAN

PERSONAL	
PROFESSIONAL	
SPIRITUAL	
EMOTIONAL	
PHYSICAL	
PSYCHOLOGICAL	

<u>WEEKLY SELF ESTEEM CHECK IN</u>

Choose 1 of the following prompts to respond to for each day of the week

SOMETHING I DID WELL WAS	I FELT PROUD WHEN
SOMETHING I DID FOR SOMEONE ELSE	I TRIED
SOMETHING I DID FOR MYSELF	I FELT GOOD ABOUT MYSELF WHEN
I HAD A GOOD EXPERIENCE WITH	I LEARNED
I ACCOMPLISHED	I CHALLENGED MYSELF TO

MONDAY:

TUESDAY:

WEDNESDAY:

THURSDAY:

FRIDAY:

SATURDAY:

SUNDAY:

SELF LOVE GROCERY LIST

As you create your grocery list for the week try to incorporate at least one food into each of the following categories to ensure you are taking care of your whole body, mind, and spirit. Plan your trips to the grocery store not just for food to eat but rather food that nourishes you. Under Meal Challenge-- think of a recipe you have been wanting to try, a food you want to cut out or add in to your diet. Do this weekly to see a drastic change in your overall health.

BRAIN FOOD	GUT HEALTH
SKIN AND HAIR CARE	SLEEP
HEALTHY INDULGENCES	HEALTHY MUNCHIES
HOUSEHOLD	MEAL CHALLENGE

<u>YOUR WEEKLY WHY</u>

Use this space to learn, grow and powerfully understand your thoughts and decision-making processes. Do this anytime you need clarity. Write it on a napkin, a back of an envelope, a journal, or anywhere you can write down and work through your thoughts.

The formula is simple.

Think of something during the week that excited you, upset you, stressed you out, made you inexplicably happy, or devastatingly sad. This could be an event, a choice, or even a conversation.

Then ask yourself WHY three times.

MY NEEDS THIS WEEK

Brainstorm your needs this week. Prioritize by number and add to your weekly calendar.

PERSONAL NEEDS:

PROFESSIONAL NEEDS:

SPIRITUAL NEEDS:

PHYSICAL NEEDS

EMOTIONAL NEEDS

PSYCHOLOGICAL NEEDS

IM POSSIBLE SELF WEEKLY SELF CARE PLAN

	MONDAY	TUESDAY	WEDNESDAY	THURSDAY	FRIDAY
PERSONAL					
PROFESSIONAL					
SPIRITUAL					
EMOTIONAL					
PHYSICAL					
PHYSICAL					

Reminders are personal mantras to be used in times of stress, decision-making, or in moments of gratitude and joy. Write your reminder for the week.

Support: Who or what will support you this week in your Self-Care goals.

REMINDERS	SUPPORT

Hmmmm...

If you talked to your friends the same way you talk to your body, would you have any friends left?

List 3 compliments you can give to your body (and say them like you mean them)

WEEKEND SELF CARE PLAN

PERSONAL	
PROFESSIONAL	
SPIRITUAL	
EMOTIONAL	
PHYSICAL	
PSYCHOLOGICAL	

WEEKLY SELF ESTEEM CHECK IN

Choose 1 of the following prompts to respond to for each day of the week

SOMETHING I DID THAT MADE ME FEEL GOOD	I TOOK CARE OF MYSELF
SOMETHING I DID FOR SOMEONE ELSE	I EXPERIENCED
SOMETHING I DID FOR MYSELF	I FELT HAPPY WHEN
I MET	I LEARNED
I ACCOMPLISHED	I CHALLENGED MYSELF TO

MONDAY:

TUESDAY:

WEDNESDAY:

THURSDAY:

FRIDAY:

SATURDAY:

SUNDAY:

SELF LOVE GROCERY LIST

As you create your grocery list for the week try to incorporate at least one food into each of the following categories to ensure you are taking care of your whole body, mind, and spirit. Plan your trips to the grocery store not just for food to eat but rather food that nourishes you. Under Meal Challenge-- think of a recipe you have been wanting to try, a food you want to cut out or add in to your diet. Do this weekly to see a drastic change in your overall health.

BRAIN FOOD	GUT HEALTH
SKIN AND HAIR CARE	**SLEEP**
HEALTHY INDULGENCES	**HEALTHY MUNCHIES**
HOUSEHOLD	**MEAL CHALLENGE**

<u>YOUR WEEKLY WHY</u>

Use this space to learn, grow and powerfully understand your thoughts and decision-making processes. Do this anytime you need clarity. Write it on a napkin, a back of an envelope, a journal, or anywhere you can write down and work through your thoughts.

The formula is simple.

Think of something during the week that excited you, upset you, stressed you out, made you inexplicably happy, or devastatingly sad. This could be an event, a choice, or even a conversation.

Then ask yourself WHY three times.

MY NEEDS THIS WEEK

Brainstorm your needs this week. Prioritize by number and add to your weekly calendar.

PERSONAL NEEDS:

PROFESSIONAL NEEDS:

SPIRITUAL NEEDS:

PHYSICAL NEEDS

EMOTIONAL NEEDS

PSYCHOLOGICAL NEEDS

When looking at my life right now, today, what do I need more of? What do I need less of?

IM POSSIBLE SELF WEEKLY SELF CARE PLAN

	MONDAY	TUESDAY	WEDNESDAY	THURSDAY	FRIDAY
PERSONAL					
PROFESSIONAL					
SPIRITUAL					
EMOTIONAL					
PHYSICAL					
PHYSICAL					

Reminders are personal mantras to be used in times of stress, decision-making, or in moments of gratitude and joy. Write your reminder for the week.

Support: Who or what will support you this week in your Self-Care goals.

REMINDERS	SUPPORT

WEEKEND SELF CARE PLAN

PERSONAL	
PROFESSIONAL	
SPIRITUAL	
EMOTIONAL	
PHYSICAL	
PSYCHOLOGICAL	

WEEKLY SELF ESTEEM CHECK IN

Choose 1 of the following prompts to respond to for each day of the week

SOMETHING I DID WELL WAS	I FELT PROUD WHEN
SOMETHING I DID FOR SOMEONE ELSE	I HEARD MY INNER VOICE WHEN
SOMETHING I HELPED ANOTHER WITH WAS	I OBEYED MY INNER VOICE WHEN
I HAD A GOOD EXPERIENCE WITH	I LEARNED
I ACCOMPLISHED	I CHALLENGED MYSELF TO

MONDAY:

TUESDAY:

WEDNESDAY:

THURSDAY:

FRIDAY:

SATURDAY:

SUNDAY:

Challenge Yourself to...

- Go to bed 30 minutes earlier than usual
- Put your phone away during meals alone. Just be with yourself.
- Before looking at social apps in the morning, open Notes and jot down 5 things you are grateful for or excited for that day.
- Unsubscribe from any junk emails cluttering your inbox and taking you away from being present
- Plan a dream vacation with a manageable time line. Start saving for it.
- Go for a walk and stop frequently just to breathe.
- Clean out your wardrobe and donate anything you do not wear.
- Change your bedsheets. Give your bedroom a facelift.
- Wander a bookstore.
- Order something out of the ordinary from the menu

SELF LOVE GROCERY LIST

As you create your grocery list for the week try to incorporate at least one food into each of the following categories to ensure you are taking care of your whole body, mind, and spirit. Plan your trips to the grocery store not just for food to eat but rather food that nourishes you. Under Meal Challenge-- think of a recipe you have been wanting to try, a food you want to cut out or add in to your diet. Do this weekly to see a drastic change in your overall health.

BRAIN FOOD	GUT HEALTH
SKIN AND HAIR CARE	SLEEP
HEALTHY INDULGENCES	HEALTHY MUNCHIES
HOUSEHOLD	MEAL CHALLENGE

YOUR WEEKLY WHY

Use this space to learn, grow and powerfully understand your thoughts and decision-making processes. Do this anytime you need clarity. Write it on a napkin, a back of an envelope, a journal, or anywhere you can write down and work through your thoughts.

The formula is simple.

Think of something during the week that excited you, upset you, stressed you out, made you inexplicably happy, or devastatingly sad. This could be an event, a choice, or even a conversation.

Then ask yourself WHY three times.

LIBERATION LETTER

Use this template to write a letter to someone or something you must release in order to move forward. This letter is meant for you to acknowledge the people, habits or activities that are no longer serving you. Use this template once a month to allow for optimal growth. Use this page or ideally a separate sheet of paper to allow for thoughtful responses.

Dear,

I am choosing to say goodbye because

You should know saying goodbye makes me feel

Because of you I have felt

I have learned

I now understand

I value

When I say goodbye to you I will no longer

You will know I have said goodbye when

Sincerely,

HELLO LETTER

Now that you have said goodbye to someone or something that has been holding you back from taking care of yourself and living abundantly, you must check in with yourself. This step is crucial as it will promote healing, create a plan to truly move forward and aid in closure. Use template once a month to allow for optimal growth. Use this page or ideally a separate sheet of paper to allow for thoughtful responses.

Dear,

I just said goodbye to

Saying goodbye to makes me feel

but I know it is for the best. Some of the reasons I know this is for the best are because

Moving forward will be hard. That is ok. Please allow yourself time to feel

Some things you can do when you feel upset about closing this chapter are

Some people you can talk to are

There will be ups and downs, good days and bad days. That is part of difficult change, and it is normal and OK. On the really hard days a reminder you can use is

On the really great days a reminder you can use is

Here are three things I feel confident I can do to move forward and say goodbye

1.

2.

3.

Lastly, thank you for acknowledging it was time to let go. Thank you for honoring your health and your spirit. You deserve the best life has to offer and I am proud of you for putting yourself first.

Love always,

5 Minute Reflection

Feelings

How did you feel this month?

What did you dream up that excited you?

What positive things did you hear?

What made you feel happy?

What did you indulge in?

What made you feel appreciated?

What did you work on to reach a future goal?

What did you spend time thinking about?

Write out a few things that you hope to feel next month:

THOUGHT FILTERING

Understanding how we think is crucial in self-discovery and self-care. Negative thinking is a normal part of human existence. It is unreasonable to believe you will never have another negative thought again. However, it is completely reasonable to believe you can learn to filter out those negative thoughts to make room for more positive rumination.

Write a negative thought you have often and then dispute it below

Sometimes I think:

But a more productive thought is:

Is my original thought backed up by evidence or backed up by emotion? (Fear, shame, guilt)

Are there any other negative thoughts you have? Write those down and then repeat the process from above. Do this exercise often. Make a habit of asking yourself if your thoughts are backed by evidence or backed by emotion (fear, guilt, shame).

GOAL DIGGER

	What am I doing well?	Where would I like to improve?	Goals	How will achieving this goal make me feel?
Intimate relationships				
Family				
Health				
Emotional Health				
Friendships				
Professional				
Education				

Intimate Relationships: Marriage, boyfriend or girlfriend

Family: People you are related to

Health: What you eat, how much you move your body, sleep...etc.

Emotional Health: Thoughts, influences, feelings

Friendships: Relationships with people you are not related to

Professional: Career goals, achievements, path

Education: School, expanding knowledge via books, documentaries, etc.

TIPS FOR SELF CARE

Professional:	**Personal:**	**Spiritual:**
Create a sensory kit. Find items that overwhelm your senses with joy; Tastes, touch, scent, sight. Have an item for each sense at your desk or workspace.	**Do your Weekly Why DAILY.** Check in with yourself daily to make sure you are making choices that represent and support the person you truly are and are becoming.	**Moon Phases** Use the moon cycles as you guide to spiritual self-care. With each full moon release wounds and set intentions.
Physical:	**Emotional:**	**Psychological:**
Face Mask The poster child of self-care. The reason face masks are so great is because not only do they help your skin look better, in turn making you feel better about your appearance, but the simple act of making time and choosing to care for skin is game changer. You are telling your body you honor it and want to nourish it.	**Be Kind, don't rewind.** In other words—begin to learn how to heal from past injuries to mind and spirit, and then how to move forward. Do not continue to revisit those wounds unless you are there to do the hard and noble work of healing them.	**Dance.** Science has proved dancing relieves stress and anxiety. That's science, you can't mess with science.

"No one else in the world can be an expert in you. Your experiences, successes, failures and relationships are uniquely yours and cannot be duplicated or replicated by anyone else in the world. No else has walked that path but you."

-Betsy Appleton

MY NEEDS THIS WEEK

Brainstorm your needs this week. Prioritize by number and add to your weekly calendar.

PERSONAL NEEDS:

PROFESSIONAL NEEDS:

SPIRITUAL NEEDS:

PHYSICAL NEEDS

EMOTIONAL NEEDS

PSYCHOLOGICAL NEEDS

IM POSSIBLE SELF WEEKLY SELF CARE PLAN

	MONDAY	TUESDAY	WEDNESDAY	THURSDAY	FRIDAY
PERSONAL					
PROFESSIONAL					
SPIRITUAL					
EMOTIONAL					
PHYSICAL					
PHYSICAL					

Reminders are personal mantras to be used in times of stress, decision-making, or in moments of gratitude and joy. Write your reminder for the week.

Support: Who or what will support you this week in your Self-Care goals.

REMINDERS	SUPPORT

The problem with putting others first is that you are teaching them you come second.

Who or what have you been putting ahead of your needs?

How can you change that and prioritize yourself?

When can you start?

WEEKEND SELF CARE PLAN

PERSONAL	
PROFESSIONAL	
SPIRITUAL	
EMOTIONAL	
PHYSICAL	
PSYCHOLOGICAL	

WEEKLY SELF ESTEEM CHECK IN

Choose 1 of the following prompts to respond to for each day of the week

I FELT GOOD WHEN	I FELT PROUD WHEN
SOMETHING I DID FOR SOMEONE ELSE	I GAVE LOVE TO
SOMETHING I DID FOR MYSELF	I FELT GOOD ABOUT MYSELF WHEN
I FACED … FEAR	I LEARNED
I MADE PROGRESS ON	I CHALLENGED MYSELF TO

MONDAY:

TUESDAY:

WEDNESDAY:

THURSDAY:

FRIDAY:

SATURDAY:

SUNDAY:

SELF LOVE GROCERY LIST

As you create your grocery list for the week try to incorporate at least one food into each of the following categories to ensure you are taking care of your whole body, mind, and spirit. Plan your trips to the grocery store not just for food to eat but rather food that nourishes you. Under Meal Challenge-- think of a recipe you have been wanting to try, a food you want to cut out or add in to your diet. Do this weekly to see a drastic change in your overall health.

BRAIN FOOD	GUT HEALTH
SKIN AND HAIR CARE	SLEEP
HEALTHY INDULGENCES	HEALTHY MUNCHIES
HOUSEHOLD	MEAL CHALLENGE

YOUR WEEKLY WHY

Use this space to learn, grow and powerfully understand your thoughts and decision-making processes. Do this anytime you need clarity. Write it on a napkin, a back of an envelope, a journal, or anywhere you can write down and work through your thoughts.

The formula is simple.

Think of something during the week that excited you, upset you, stressed you out, made you inexplicably happy, or devastatingly sad. This could be an event, a choice, or even a conversation.

Then ask yourself WHY three times.

MY NEEDS THIS WEEK

Brainstorm your needs this week. Prioritize by number and add to your weekly calendar.

PERSONAL NEEDS:

PROFESSIONAL NEEDS:

SPIRITUAL NEEDS:

PHYSICAL NEEDS

EMOTIONAL NEEDS

PSYCHOLOGICAL NEEDS

IM POSSIBLE SELF WEEKLY SELF CARE PLAN

	MONDAY	TUESDAY	WEDNESDAY	THURSDAY	FRIDAY
PERSONAL					
PROFESSIONAL					
SPIRITUAL					
EMOTIONAL					
PHYSICAL					
PHYSICAL					

Reminders are personal mantras to be used in times of stress, decision-making, or in moments of gratitude and joy. Write your reminder for the week.

Support: Who or what will support you this week in your Self-Care goals.

REMINDERS	SUPPORT

WEEKEND SELF CARE PLAN

PERSONAL	
PROFESSIONAL	
SPIRITUAL	
EMOTIONAL	
PHYSICAL	
PSYCHOLOGICAL	

WEEKLY SELF ESTEEM CHECK IN

Choose 1 of the following prompts to respond to for each day of the week

I SPOKE KINDLY TO MYSELF WHEN	I FELT PROUD WHEN
SOMETHING I DID FOR SOMEONE ELSE	I TRIED
SOMETHING I DID FOR MYSELF	I FELT GOOD ABOUT MYSELF WHEN
I FELT INSPIRED BY	I LEARNED
I ACCOMPLISHED	I CHALLENGED MYSELF TO

MONDAY:

TUESDAY:

WEDNESDAY:

THURSDAY:

FRIDAY:

SATURDAY:

SUNDAY:

SELF LOVE GROCERY LIST

As you create your grocery list for the week try to incorporate at least one food into each of the following categories to ensure you are taking care of your whole body, mind, and spirit. Plan your trips to the grocery store not just for food to eat but rather food that nourishes you. Under Meal Challenge-- think of a recipe you have been wanting to try, a food you want to cut out or add in to your diet. Do this weekly to see a drastic change in your overall health.

BRAIN FOOD	GUT HEALTH
SKIN AND HAIR CARE	SLEEP
HEALTHY INDULGENCES	HEALTHY MUNCHIES
HOUSEHOLD	MEAL CHALLENGE

YOUR WEEKLY WHY

Use this space to learn, grow and powerfully understand your thoughts and decision-making processes. Do this anytime you need clarity. Write it on a napkin, a back of an envelope, a journal, or anywhere you can write down and work through your thoughts.

The formula is simple.

Think of something during the week that excited you, upset you, stressed you out, made you inexplicably happy, or devastatingly sad. This could be an event, a choice, or even a conversation.

Then ask yourself WHY three times.

MY NEEDS THIS WEEK

Brainstorm your needs this week. Prioritize by number and add to your weekly calendar.

PERSONAL NEEDS:

PROFESSIONAL NEEDS:

SPIRITUAL NEEDS:

PHYSICAL NEEDS

EMOTIONAL NEEDS

PSYCHOLOGICAL NEEDS

When change occurs inside of you, change will occur outside of you.

What changes have you noticed internally since you began using this planning guide? What changes externally have you noticed as a result?

IM POSSIBLE SELF WEEKLY SELF CARE PLAN

	MONDAY	TUESDAY	WEDNESDAY	THURSDAY	FRIDAY
PERSONAL					
PROFESSIONAL					
SPIRITUAL					
EMOTIONAL					
PHYSICAL					
PHYSICAL					

Reminders are personal mantras to be used in times of stress, decision-making, or in moments of gratitude and joy. Write your reminder for the week.

Support: Who or what will support you this week in your Self-Care goals.

REMINDERS	SUPPORT

WEEKEND SELF CARE PLAN

PERSONAL	
PROFESSIONAL	
SPIRITUAL	
EMOTIONAL	
PHYSICAL	
PSYCHOLOGICAL	

WEEKLY SELF ESTEEM CHECK IN

Choose 1 of the following prompts to respond to for each day of the week

SOMETHING I DID WELL WAS	I FELT PROUD WHEN
SOMETHING I DID FOR SOMEONE ELSE	I TRIED
SOMETHING I DID FOR MYSELF	I FELT GOOD ABOUT MYSELF WHEN
I HAD A GOOD EXPERIENCE WITH	I LEARNED
I ACCOMPLISHED	I CHALLENGED MYSELF TO

MONDAY:

TUESDAY:

WEDNESDAY:

THURSDAY:

FRIDAY:

SATURDAY:

SUNDAY:

SELF LOVE GROCERY LIST

As you create your grocery list for the week try to incorporate at least one food into each of the following categories to ensure you are taking care of your whole body, mind, and spirit. Plan your trips to the grocery store not just for food to eat but rather food that nourishes you. Under Meal Challenge-- think of a recipe you have been wanting to try, a food you want to cut out or add in to your diet. Do this weekly to see a drastic change in your overall health.

BRAIN FOOD	GUT HEALTH
SKIN AND HAIR CARE	SLEEP
HEALTHY INDULGENCES	HEALTHY MUNCHIES
HOUSEHOLD	MEAL CHALLENGE

<u>YOUR WEEKLY WHY</u>

Use this space to learn, grow and powerfully understand your thoughts and decision-making processes. Do this anytime you need clarity. Write it on a napkin, a back of an envelope, a journal, or anywhere you can write down and work through your thoughts.

The formula is simple.

Think of something during the week that excited you, upset you, stressed you out, made you inexplicably happy, or devastatingly sad. This could be an event, a choice, or even a conversation.

Then ask yourself WHY three times.

MY NEEDS THIS WEEK

Brainstorm your needs this week. Prioritize by number and add to your weekly calendar.

PERSONAL NEEDS:

PROFESSIONAL NEEDS:

SPIRITUAL NEEDS:

PHYSICAL NEEDS

EMOTIONAL NEEDS

PSYCHOLOGICAL NEEDS

IM POSSIBLE SELF WEEKLY SELF CARE PLAN

	MONDAY	TUESDAY	WEDNESDAY	THURSDAY	FRIDAY
PERSONAL					
PROFESSIONAL					
SPIRITUAL					
EMOTIONAL					
PHYSICAL					
PHYSICAL					

Reminders are personal mantras to be used in times of stress, decision-making, or in moments of gratitude and joy. Write your reminder for the week.

Support: Who or what will support you this week in your Self-Care goals.

REMINDERS	SUPPORT

WEEKEND SELF CARE PLAN

PERSONAL	
PROFESSIONAL	
SPIRITUAL	
EMOTIONAL	
PHYSICAL	
PSYCHOLOGICAL	

WEEKLY SELF ESTEEM CHECK IN

Choose 1 of the following prompts to respond to for each day of the week

SOMETHING I TRIED	I FELT PROUD WHEN
SOMETHING I DID FOR SOMEONE ELSE	I LISTENED TO MY INNER VOICE WHEN
SOMETHING I DID FOR MYSELF	I FELT GOOD ABOUT MYSELF WHEN
I IGNORED	I LEARNED
I ACCOMPLISHED	I CHALLENGED MYSELF TO

MONDAY:

TUESDAY:

WEDNESDAY:

THURSDAY:

FRIDAY:

SATURDAY:

SUNDAY:

SELF LOVE GROCERY LIST

As you create your grocery list for the week try to incorporate at least one food into each of the following categories to ensure you are taking care of your whole body, mind, and spirit. Plan your trips to the grocery store not just for food to eat but rather food that nourishes you. Under Meal Challenge-- think of a recipe you have been wanting to try, a food you want to cut out or add in to your diet. Do this weekly to see a drastic change in your overall health.

BRAIN FOOD	GUT HEALTH
SKIN AND HAIR CARE	SLEEP
HEALTHY INDULGENCES	HEALTHY MUNCHIES
HOUSEHOLD	MEAL CHALLENGE

Life is too short to spend it at war with yourself.

What battle can you surrender to today?

<u>YOUR WEEKLY WHY</u>

Use this space to learn, grow and powerfully understand your thoughts and decision-making processes. Do this anytime you need clarity. Write it on a napkin, a back of an envelope, a journal, or anywhere you can write down and work through your thoughts.

The formula is simple.

Think of something during the week that excited you, upset you, stressed you out, made you inexplicably happy, or devastatingly sad. This could be an event, a choice, or even a conversation.

Then ask yourself WHY three times.

LIBERATION LETTER

Use this template to write a letter to someone or something you must release in order to move forward. This letter is meant for you to acknowledge the people, habits or activities that are no longer serving you. Use this template once a month to allow for optimal growth. Use this page or ideally a separate sheet of paper to allow for thoughtful responses.

Dear,

I am choosing to say goodbye because

You should know saying goodbye makes me feel

I would like to thank you for

You taught me

You showed me

You gave me

When I say goodbye to you I will no longer

I believe when I let you go, I will feel

Sincerely,

HELLO LETTER

Now that you have said goodbye to someone or something that has been holding you back from taking care of yourself and living abundantly, you must check in with yourself. This step is crucial as it will promote healing, create a plan to truly move forward and aid in closure. Use template once a month to allow for optimal growth. Use this page or ideally a separate sheet of paper to allow for thoughtful responses.

Dear,

I just said goodbye to

Saying goodbye to makes me feel

but I know it is for the best. Some of the reasons I know this is for the best are because

Moving forward will be hard. That is ok. Please allow yourself time to feel

Some things you can do when you feel upset about closing this chapter are

Some people you can talk to are

There will be ups and downs, good days and bad days. That is part of difficult change, and it is normal and OK. On the really hard days a reminder you can use is

On the really great days a reminder you can use is

Here are three things I feel confident I can do to move forward and say goodbye

1.

2.

3.

Lastly, thank you for acknowledging it was time to let go. Thank you for honoring your health and your spirit. You deserve the best life has to offer and I am proud of you for putting yourself first.

Love always,

LET'S MAKE A PLAN

PERSONAL RESCOUCRES

Take a few minutes to brainstorm healthy ways you can express or cope with emotions. Use this as your personal resource whenever you feel stuck in an emotion.

When I am angry

When I am sad

When I feel scared

When I need to vent

When I am triggered by a past pain

When I feel anxious

Brainstorm the things that bring you the most joy. Use this as a resource anytime you want to do something to lift your spirits or simply to feel an abundance of joy.

What or who makes me laugh the hardest?

When do I feel most alive?

What makes me smile so much my face hurts?

Write down three of your happiest memories. How can you recreate those? Are there elements you can bring into your life right now?

5 Minute Reflection

Connection

For the next five minutes answer in words, phrases, names or drawings the following:

What makes you feel most connected to your truest self?

What makes you feel the most disconnected from your truest self?

NO THANK YOU

Burn out. It happens. In fact, it happens often. Many times, burn out occurs from taking on more than we can handle. Usually we do not realize we are overloading ourselves until we crumble beneath the weight. This activity will help you sort through what you can carry and what is not yours to hold.

List everything on your plate:

Of the items listed above what are other people's responsibilities that you have taken on?

Of the items listed above, which drain you the most mentally?

Which drain you the most physically?

Are there any items that really do not need to get done? Or items you can push to the bottom of your To-Do List?

How is the above list affecting your needs being met?

Choose items from above you would feel comfortable asking for help with. This is the hardest part, but the most necessary. Practice letting go of guilt and speak your need. It can be as small as asking your spouse to fold the laundry this time, or as big as telling a friend you cannot attend an event you committed yourself to.

What can you remind yourself of as you ask for help? (Example: "I am not failing by not being able to do everything. In asking for help I am taking care of myself and it allows me to do the most important things better. Asking for help with these things is actually allowing me to be more successful. I deserve that, and the people I am continuing to help deserve the best of me and that can only happen if I ask for help with this load."

TIPS FOR SELF CARE

Professional:	Personal:	Spiritual:
Commute perspective shift Commuting is a drag for several reasons. It is typically slow; you often aren't super excited about where you are headed and it can cause a lot of anxiety. Try to shift your perspective to see that time in car or on train as "me time." We are constantly surrounded by people and expected to engage, think of the commute as a silent time made just for you.	**Unplug.** Not just on social media, but TV as well. Remove images and influence that distract you from the goodness of you, makes you feel less or causes you distress.	**Breathe Work** When you focus on your breathing it immediately brings you inward which allows for your inner voice to be heard and valued. The more you get to know that voice the more you will get to know yourself and how to take care of yourself appropriately.
Physical:	**Emotional:**	**Psychological:**
Stretch Did you know Hip Flexor stretches will help reduce the appearance of lower belly pooch? it is true! Practice these stretches daily for a better range of motion, reduced back pain and to get rid of your lower belly.	**Animal Instincts** Visit your local shelter, borrow a friend's dog or visit a cat café. spending time with animals is proven to boost mood and emotional wellbeing.	**Book Club** Treat your mind to a new book. learn something or dive into a whole new world. Your brain needs nourishment just as the rest of your body does.

"Take time to move; it is what your body was made to do,

To think; it is your source o power

To play; it is the secret to eternal YOUth

To read; it is wisdom passed down

To pray; it is the best WiFi connection

To love; it is a blessed gift

To be friendly; it is the road to happiness

To laugh; it is the music of the soul

To give; it is heaven in the present

--Daisy Alexandria

MY NEEDS THIS WEEK

Brainstorm your needs this week. Prioritize by number and add to your weekly calendar.

PERSONAL NEEDS:

PROFESSIONAL NEEDS:

SPIRITUAL NEEDS:

PHYSICAL NEEDS

EMOTIONAL NEEDS

PSYCHOLOGICAL NEEDS

IM POSSIBLE SELF WEEKLY SELF CARE PLAN

	MONDAY	TUESDAY	WEDNESDAY	THURSDAY	FRIDAY
PERSONAL					
PROFESSIONAL					
SPIRITUAL					
EMOTIONAL					
PHYSICAL					
PHYSICAL					

Reminders are personal mantras to be used in times of stress, decision-making, or in moments of gratitude and joy. Write your reminder for the week.

Support: Who or what will support you this week in your Self-Care goals.

REMINDERS	SUPPORT

WEEKEND SELF CARE PLAN

PERSONAL	
PROFESSIONAL	
SPIRITUAL	
EMOTIONAL	
PHYSICAL	
PSYCHOLOGICAL	

WEEKLY SELF ESTEEM CHECK IN

Choose 1 of the following prompts to respond to for each day of the week

SOMETHING I DID WELL WAS	I FELT PROUD WHEN
SOMETHING I DID FOR SOMEONE ELSE	I LISTENED TO
SOMETHING I DID FOR MYSELF	I FELT GOOD ABOUT MYSELF WHEN
I GOT INVOLVED IN	I TRIED TO UNDERSTAND
I GAVE BACK TO	I CHALLENGED MYSELF TO

MONDAY:

TUESDAY:

WEDNESDAY:

THURSDAY:

FRIDAY:

SATURDAY:

SUNDAY:

SELF LOVE GROCERY LIST

As you create your grocery list for the week try to incorporate at least one food into each of the following categories to ensure you are taking care of your whole body, mind, and spirit. Plan your trips to the grocery store not just for food to eat but rather food that nourishes you. Under Meal Challenge-- think of a recipe you have been wanting to try, a food you want to cut out or add in to your diet. Do this weekly to see a drastic change in your overall health.

BRAIN FOOD	GUT HEALTH
SKIN AND HAIR CARE	SLEEP
HEALTHY INDULGENCES	HEALTHY MUNCHIES
HOUSEHOLD	MEAL CHALLENGE

<u>YOUR WEEKLY WHY</u>

Use this space to learn, grow and powerfully understand your thoughts and decision-making processes. Do this anytime you need clarity. Write it on a napkin, a back of an envelope, a journal, or anywhere you can write down and work through your thoughts.

The formula is simple.

Think of something during the week that excited you, upset you, stressed you out, made you inexplicably happy, or devastatingly sad. This could be an event, a choice, or even a conversation.

Then ask yourself WHY three times.

MY NEEDS THIS WEEK

Brainstorm your needs this week. Prioritize by number and add to your weekly calendar.

PERSONAL NEEDS:

PROFESSIONAL NEEDS:

SPIRITUAL NEEDS:

PHYSICAL NEEDS

EMOTIONAL NEEDS

PSYCHOLOGICAL NEEDS

IM POSSIBLE SELF WEEKLY SELF CARE PLAN

	MONDAY	TUESDAY	WEDNESDAY	THURSDAY	FRIDAY
PERSONAL					
PROFESSIONAL					
SPIRITUAL					
EMOTIONAL					
PHYSICAL					
PHYSICAL					

Reminders are personal mantras to be used in times of stress, decision-making, or in moments of gratitude and joy. Write your reminder for the week.

Support: Who or what will support you this week in your Self-Care goals.

REMINDERS	SUPPORT

WEEKEND SELF CARE PLAN

PERSONAL	
PROFESSIONAL	
SPIRITUAL	
EMOTIONAL	
PHYSICAL	
PSYCHOLOGICAL	

WEEKLY SELF ESTEEM CHECK IN

Choose 1 of the following prompts to respond to for each day of the week

I MADE SOMEONE HAPPY WHEN	I FELT PROUD WHEN
I PAID IT FORWARD BY	I MADE PROGRESS ON
SOMETHING I DID FOR MYSELF	I FELT GOOD ABOUT MYSELF WHEN
A COMPLIMENT I GAVE WAS	I LEARNED
I ACCOMPLISHED	I CHALLENGED MYSELF TO

MONDAY:

TUESDAY:

WEDNESDAY:

THURSDAY:

FRIDAY:

SATURDAY:

SUNDAY:

Beware of destination addiction.

We are programmed to believe that happiness is in the next place, the next phase, the next job, the next house, the next relationship, the next lowest number on the scale.

Until you release the idea that happiness is somewhere else, somewhere outside of you, happiness will NEVER be where you are.

Magic flows from the present. Embrace who you are. Love who you are right now.

SELF LOVE GROCERY LIST

As you create your grocery list for the week try to incorporate at least one food into each of the following categories to ensure you are taking care of your whole body, mind, and spirit. Plan your trips to the grocery store not just for food to eat but rather food that nourishes you. Under Meal Challenge-- think of a recipe you have been wanting to try, a food you want to cut out or add in to your diet. Do this weekly to see a drastic change in your overall health.

BRAIN FOOD	GUT HEALTH
SKIN AND HAIR CARE	**SLEEP**
HEALTHY INDULGENCES	**HEALTHY MUNCHIES**
HOUSEHOLD	**MEAL CHALLENGE**

YOUR WEEKLY WHY

Use this space to learn, grow and powerfully understand your thoughts and decision-making processes. Do this anytime you need clarity. Write it on a napkin, a back of an envelope, a journal, or anywhere you can write down and work through your thoughts.

The formula is simple.

Think of something during the week that excited you, upset you, stressed you out, made you inexplicably happy, or devastatingly sad. This could be an event, a choice, or even a conversation.

Then ask yourself WHY three times.

MY NEEDS THIS WEEK

Brainstorm your needs this week. Prioritize by number and add to your weekly calendar.

PERSONAL NEEDS:

PROFESSIONAL NEEDS:

SPIRITUAL NEEDS:

PHYSICAL NEEDS

EMOTIONAL NEEDS

PSYCHOLOGICAL NEEDS

IM POSSIBLE SELF WEEKLY SELF CARE PLAN

	MONDAY	TUESDAY	WEDNESDAY	THURSDAY	FRIDAY
PERSONAL					
PROFESSIONAL					
SPIRITUAL					
EMOTIONAL					
PHYSICAL					
PHYSICAL					

Reminders are personal mantras to be used in times of stress, decision-making, or in moments of gratitude and joy. Write your reminder for the week.

Support: Who or what will support you this week in your Self-Care goals.

REMINDERS	SUPPORT

WEEKEND SELF CARE PLAN

PERSONAL	
PROFESSIONAL	
SPIRITUAL	
EMOTIONAL	
PHYSICAL	
PSYCHOLOGICAL	

WEEKLY SELF ESTEEM CHECK IN

Choose 1 of the following prompts to respond to for each day of the week

SOMETHING I GAVE MY ATTENTION TO	I FELT HAPPY WHEN
SOMETHING I DID FOR SOMEONE ELSE	I EXPLORED
SOMETHING I DID FOR MYSELF	I FELT GOOD ABOUT MYSELF WHEN
I HAD A GOOD TIME WITH	I TOOK CARE OF MYSELF BY
I ACCOMPLISHED	I CHALLENGED MYSELF TO

MONDAY:

TUESDAY:

WEDNESDAY:

THURSDAY:

FRIDAY:

SATURDAY:

SUNDAY:

SELF LOVE GROCERY LIST

As you create your grocery list for the week try to incorporate at least one food into each of the following categories to ensure you are taking care of your whole body, mind, and spirit. Plan your trips to the grocery store not just for food to eat but rather food that nourishes you. Under Meal Challenge-- think of a recipe you have been wanting to try, a food you want to cut out or add in to your diet. Do this weekly to see a drastic change in your overall health.

BRAIN FOOD	GUT HEALTH
SKIN AND HAIR CARE	**SLEEP**
HEALTHY INDULGENCES	**HEALTHY MUNCHIES**
HOUSEHOLD	**MEAL CHALLENGE**

BEETS

Beets have a strong flavor that many avoid, but if you know how to cook them, they can be a delicious and healthy treat. Beets improve liver function, reduce inflammation, improve stamina, combat anemia, lower blood pressure, are fantastic for digestion, and boost your immunity.

Try Beet Tacos!

(trust me)

- 1lb beets, peeled and quartered (Try Love Beets. They are already cooked, quartered and ready to go!)
- 1 teaspoon cumin powder (Cumin is smoky. Think Mexican chili flavors).
- Dash of salt
- 1/2 teaspoon chili powder
- 1/4 teaspoon cayenne pepper
- 2 tablespoon olive or coconut oil
- 1 avocado
- 1/4 cup low-fat Greek yogurt
- Juice from 1 lime
- Goat cheese
- Arugula
- Corn tortillas or flour tortillas. Whatever is your favorite!
- Fresh cilantro for garnish

Mix Greek yogurt, salt, pepper, lime juice in a bowl.

Dust beets with seasonings listed and mix until all the beets are evenly coated.

In a tortilla put arugula and beets. Add sliced avocado. Crumble goat cheese on top and add a dollop of the lime Greek yogurt. Garnish with cilantro.

For an added kick toss in some mandarin orange slices.

Need more substance: Add corn and black beans!

A very fresh, very healthy, easy way to enjoy beets!

<u>YOUR WEEKLY WHY</u>

Use this space to learn, grow and powerfully understand your thoughts and decision-making processes. Do this anytime you need clarity. Write it on a napkin, a back of an envelope, a journal, or anywhere you can write down and work through your thoughts.

The formula is simple.

Think of something during the week that excited you, upset you, stressed you out, made you inexplicably happy, or devastatingly sad. This could be an event, a choice, or even a conversation.

Then ask yourself WHY three times.

MY NEEDS THIS WEEK

Brainstorm your needs this week. Prioritize by number and add to your weekly calendar.

PERSONAL NEEDS:

PROFESSIONAL NEEDS:

SPIRITUAL NEEDS:

PHYSICAL NEEDS

EMOTIONAL NEEDS

PSYCHOLOGICAL NEEDS

IM POSSIBLE SELF WEEKLY SELF CARE PLAN

	MONDAY	TUESDAY	WEDNESDAY	THURSDAY	FRIDAY
PERSONAL					
PROFESSIONAL					
SPIRITUAL					
EMOTIONAL					
PHYSICAL					
PHYSICAL					

Reminders are personal mantras to be used in times of stress, decision-making, or in moments of gratitude and joy. Write your reminder for the week.

Support: Who or what will support you this week in your Self-Care goals.

REMINDERS	SUPPORT

WEEKEND SELF CARE PLAN

PERSONAL	
PROFESSIONAL	
SPIRITUAL	
EMOTIONAL	
PHYSICAL	
PSYCHOLOGICAL	

WEEKLY SELF ESTEEM CHECK IN

Choose 1 of the following prompts to respond to for each day of the week

SOMETHING I DID WELL WAS	I FELT PROUD WHEN
SOMETHING I DID FOR SOMEONE ELSE	I TRIED
SOMETHING I DID FOR MYSELF	I FELT GOOD ABOUT MYSELF WHEN
I HAD A GOOD EXPERIENCE WITH	I LEARNED
I ACCOMPLISHED	I CHALLENGED MYSELF TO

MONDAY:

TUESDAY:

WEDNESDAY:

THURSDAY:

FRIDAY:

SATURDAY:

SUNDAY:

Masks

At one time or another, in all of our lives, we have worn a mask. Masks are used for protection or for conformity. Unfortunately, when we hide behind a mask, we hide our true self from the world...and subsequently we hide from ourselves. The longer we wear the mask the more we try to conform our identity to it. But the mask will never fit just right. After a while the mask becomes uncomfortable. It may even hurt to wear. Sometimes it is only when the mask becomes unbearable that we realize we put on a mask in the first place.

Think of a mask as what you show to the world. This can be via actions, clothes, the words you use, hobbies, or even how you display your life on social media.

Ask yourself:

How many masks have you worn in your life?

What were the reason you put the mask on?

When did you realize the mask didn't fit you?

How did the mask hurt you?

Are you wearing any mask now?

How might your life be better if you removed the mask?

What is something you can do today to start removing that mask?

SELF LOVE GROCERY LIST

As you create your grocery list for the week try to incorporate at least one food into each of the following categories to ensure you are taking care of your whole body, mind, and spirit. Plan your trips to the grocery store not just for food to eat but rather food that nourishes you. Under Meal Challenge-- think of a recipe you have been wanting to try, a food you want to cut out or add in to your diet. Do this weekly to see a drastic change in your overall health.

BRAIN FOOD	GUT HEALTH
SKIN AND HAIR CARE	**SLEEP**
HEALTHY INDULGENCES	**HEALTHY MUNCHIES**
HOUSEHOLD	**MEAL CHALLENGE**

YOUR WEEKLY WHY

Use this space to learn, grow and powerfully understand your thoughts and decision-making processes. Do this anytime you need clarity. Write it on a napkin, a back of an envelope, a journal, or anywhere you can write down and work through your thoughts.

The formula is simple.

Think of something during the week that excited you, upset you, stressed you out, made you inexplicably happy, or devastatingly sad. This could be an event, a choice, or even a conversation.

Then ask yourself WHY three times.

LIBERATION LETTER

Use this template to write a letter to someone or something you must release in order to move forward. This letter is meant for you to acknowledge the people, habits or activities that are no longer serving you. Use this template once a month to allow for optimal growth. Use this page or ideally a separate sheet of paper to allow for thoughtful responses.

Dear,

I am choosing to say goodbye because

You should know saying goodbye makes me feel

In the time we had together I learned

You showed me

I have begun to value

I know that now I must

When I say goodbye to you I will no longer

Sincerely,

HELLO LETTER

Now that you have said goodbye to someone or something that has been holding you back from taking care of yourself and living abundantly, you must check in with yourself. This step is crucial as it will promote healing, create a plan to truly move forward and aid in closure. Use template once a month to allow for optimal growth. Use this page or ideally a separate sheet of paper or blank sheets in back of planner to allow for thoughtful responses.

Dear,

I just said goodbye to

Saying goodbye to makes me feel

but I know it is for the best. Some of the reasons I know this is for the best are because

Moving forward will be hard. That is ok. Please allow yourself time to feel

Some things you can do when you feel upset about closing this chapter are

Some people you can talk to are

There will be ups and downs, good days and bad days. That is part of difficult change, and it is normal and OK. On the really hard days a reminder you can use is

On the really great days a reminder you can use is

Here are three things I feel confident I can do to move forward and say goodbye

1.

2.

3.

Lastly, thank you for acknowledging it was time to let go. Thank you for honoring your health and your spirit. You deserve the best life has to offer and I am proud of you for putting yourself first.

Love always,

SHOWER THOUGHTS

We do not always have time to journal. That is OK. But chances are you have time to shower. Use that time to reflect and think about the following prompts.

3 things I love about life right now

Something I feel strongly about and want to take action on

3 things I want to do less of

What were some highs and lows of the last few days? How can I recreate the highs?

What advice could I give myself right now?

Is there anything I need to release?

Are there patterns in my life I have created that I do not like?

How can I declutter my mind?

Who or what inspired me this week?

What did I spend the most time looking at or listening to? Did this thing affect my mood in a positive or negative way?

5 Minute Reflection

Looking Ahead

What is on your To-Do list next month

What are you looking forward to?

Which item is your top priority? Why?

What challenges might you face on that list?

How will you manage those challenges?

What are a few things you can do today to make tomorrow easier?

Effective Communication

In order to have our emotional, physical and professional needs met we must be able to communicate what we need. This is often harder than it should be. When we do not properly communicate, we end up feeling ignored, betrayed and misunderstood. Here is a SIMPLE prompt for effective communication.

Try this method next time you speak your needs.

Remember, a conversation is an articulation of an emotion or need and it is coming directly from your heart. Therefore, your words should be focused on YOU.

AVOID

- **You statements:** "You do not listen to me"
- **Permanent Words:** Never and always should be avoided at all costs because those words imply the person you are speaking to is incapable of meeting your needs. "You never listen to me."

TRY THIS

I feel (insert emotion) when (insert action). I would like (insert proposed solution). That would (insert the solution explanation)

Example: "I feel ignored when you are on your phone when I am talking to you. I would like it if you could put your phone away during conversations. That would let me know that your attention is focused on what I am saying."

See the difference? The first way is accusatory and can be heard as nagging, rude or challenging. The second way is focused on how you are feeling about the behavior, there is no language that can be heard as accusing, challenging or in a nagging tone. It is a clear expression of your need backed by a possible solution. If the solution does not work for the other person, this approach opens the dialogue to a sensible, peaceful, effective conversation that may produce another amicable solution to meeting your need.

TIPS FOR SELF CARE

Professional:	Personal:	Spiritual:
Find your work tribe. Make a separate time for the people in your professional life who lift you, connect with you and value your goals, dreams and work ethic. Work friends and professional allies are vital.	**Dial** When was the last time you called a friend? Pick up the phone and call that friend you only text or talk to on social media. Have a conversation and notice how slowing down and making that time transforms your communication skills and creates space for more meaningful connections.	**Earthing** Spend 30 minutes a day with Mother Earth. Walk barefoot, swim in a lake, river or ocean, work in the garden.
Physical:	**Emotional:**	**Psychological:**
Don't be the smelly kid. Balance your body's pH with foods like cranberries, sweet potatoes, probiotic rich foods, Omega-3' fatty acids, apples, soy, avocados and dark leafy greens.	**Complete the sentence** I love myself because...	**Ask.** Practice asking for help. Hate asking for help? Start small. Notice how asking for and receiving help makes you feel nurtured rather than lacking.

"The most humbling, freeing and challenging life lesson on this conscious growth journey is that the only person responsible for my happiness is me. It is so natual to want others to behave a certain way in order for me to be happy but surrendering to the fact that they never will keeps me in my own lane and makes for way less drama."

    -Claire Byrne

MY NEEDS THIS WEEK

Brainstorm your needs this week. Prioritize by number and add to your weekly calendar.

PERSONAL NEEDS:

PROFESSIONAL NEEDS:

SPIRITUAL NEEDS:

PHYSICAL NEEDS

EMOTIONAL NEEDS

PSYCHOLOGICAL NEEDS

IM POSSIBLE SELF WEEKLY SELF CARE PLAN

	MONDAY	TUESDAY	WEDNESDAY	THURSDAY	FRIDAY
PERSONAL					
PROFESSIONAL					
SPIRITUAL					
EMOTIONAL					
PHYSICAL					
PHYSICAL					

Reminders are personal mantras to be used in times of stress, decision-making, or in moments of gratitude and joy. Write your reminder for the week.

Support: Who or what will support you this week in your Self-Care goals.

REMINDERS	SUPPORT

WEEKEND SELF CARE PLAN

PERSONAL	
PROFESSIONAL	
SPIRITUAL	
EMOTIONAL	
PHYSICAL	
PSYCHOLOGICAL	

<u>WEEKLY SELF ESTEEM CHECK IN</u>

Choose 1 of the following prompts to respond to for each day of the week

SOMETHING I SAID THAT UPLIFTED ME WAS	I ADVOCATED FOR MYSELF WHEN
SOMETHING I DID FOR SOMEONE ELSE	I SAID NO TO
SOMETHING I DID FOR MYSELF	I FELT GOOD ABOUT MYSELF WHEN
I HAD A GOOD EXPERIENCE WITH	I SAID YES TO
I ACCOMPLISHED	I CHALLENGED MYSELF TO

MONDAY:

TUESDAY:

WEDNESDAY:

THURSDAY:

FRIDAY:

SATURDAY:

SUNDAY:

SELF LOVE GROCERY LIST

     As you create your grocery list for the week try to incorporate at least one food into each of the following categories to ensure you are taking care of your whole body, mind, and spirit. Plan your trips to the grocery store not just for food to eat but rather food that nourishes you. Under Meal Challenge-- think of a recipe you have been wanting to try, a food you want to cut out or add in to your diet. Do this weekly to see a drastic change in your overall health.

BRAIN FOOD	GUT HEALTH
SKIN AND HAIR CARE	**SLEEP**
HEALTHY INDULGENCES	**HEALTHY MUNCHIES**
HOUSEHOLD	**MEAL CHALLENGE**

YOUR WEEKLY WHY

Use this space to learn, grow and powerfully understand your thoughts and decision-making processes. Do this anytime you need clarity. Write it on a napkin, a back of an envelope, a journal, or anywhere you can write down and work through your thoughts.

The formula is simple.

Think of something during the week that excited you, upset you, stressed you out, made you inexplicably happy, or devastatingly sad. This could be an event, a choice, or even a conversation.

Then ask yourself WHY three times.

MY NEEDS THIS WEEK

Brainstorm your needs this week. Prioritize by number and add to your weekly calendar.

PERSONAL NEEDS:

PROFESSIONAL NEEDS:

SPIRITUAL NEEDS:

PHYSICAL NEEDS

EMOTIONAL NEEDS

PSYCHOLOGICAL NEEDS

IM POSSIBLE SELF WEEKLY SELF CARE PLAN

	MONDAY	TUESDAY	WEDNESDAY	THURSDAY	FRIDAY
PERSONAL					
PROFESSIONAL					
SPIRITUAL					
EMOTIONAL					
PHYSICAL					
PHYSICAL					

Reminders are personal mantras to be used in times of stress, decision-making, or in moments of gratitude and joy. Write your reminder for the week.

Support: Who or what will support you this week in your Self-Care goals.

REMINDERS	SUPPORT

WEEKEND SELF CARE PLAN

PERSONAL	
PROFESSIONAL	
SPIRITUAL	
EMOTIONAL	
PHYSICAL	
PSYCHOLOGICAL	

WEEKLY SELF ESTEEM CHECK IN

Choose 1 of the following prompts to respond to for each day of the week

SOMETHING I SMILED ABOUT	I FELT PROUD WHEN
SOMETHING I DID FOR SOMEONE ELSE	I TRIED
SOMETHING I DID FOR MYSELF	I FELT GOOD ABOUT MYSELF WHEN
I PAMPERED MYSELF WITH	I ACTED KINDLY TOWARDS MYSELF WHEN
I ACCOMPLISHED	I CHALLENGED MYSELF TO

MONDAY:

TUESDAY:

WEDNESDAY:

THURSDAY:

FRIDAY:

SATURDAY:

SUNDAY:

SELF LOVE GROCERY LIST

As you create your grocery list for the week try to incorporate at least one food into each of the following categories to ensure you are taking care of your whole body, mind, and spirit. Plan your trips to the grocery store not just for food to eat but rather food that nourishes you. Under Meal Challenge-- think of a recipe you have been wanting to try, a food you want to cut out or add in to your diet. Do this weekly to see a drastic change in your overall health.

BRAIN FOOD	GUT HEALTH
SKIN AND HAIR CARE	**SLEEP**
HEALTHY INDULGENCES	**HEALTHY MUNCHIES**
HOUSEHOLD	**MEAL CHALLENGE**

<u>YOUR WEEKLY WHY</u>

Use this space to learn, grow and powerfully understand your thoughts and decision-making processes. Do this anytime you need clarity. Write it on a napkin, a back of an envelope, a journal, or anywhere you can write down and work through your thoughts.

The formula is simple.

Think of something during the week that excited you, upset you, stressed you out, made you inexplicably happy, or devastatingly sad. This could be an event, a choice, or even a conversation.

Then ask yourself WHY three times.

<u>MY NEEDS THIS WEEK</u>

Brainstorm your needs this week. Prioritize by number and add to your weekly calendar.

PERSONAL NEEDS:

PROFESSIONAL NEEDS:

SPIRITUAL NEEDS:

PHYSICAL NEEDS

EMOTIONAL NEEDS

PSYCHOLOGICAL NEEDS

IM POSSIBLE SELF WEEKLY SELF CARE PLAN

	MONDAY	TUESDAY	WEDNESDAY	THURSDAY	FRIDAY
PERSONAL					
PROFESSIONAL					
SPIRITUAL					
EMOTIONAL					
PHYSICAL					
PHYSICAL					

Reminders are personal mantras to be used in times of stress, decision-making, or in moments of gratitude and joy. Write your reminder for the week.

Support: Who or what will support you this week in your Self-Care goals.

REMINDERS	SUPPORT

WEEKEND SELF CARE PLAN

PERSONAL	
PROFESSIONAL	
SPIRITUAL	
EMOTIONAL	
PHYSICAL	
PSYCHOLOGICAL	

WEEKLY SELF ESTEEM CHECK IN

Choose 1 of the following prompts to respond to for each day of the week

SOMETHING I DID THAT MADE A POSITIVE IMPACT WAS	I FELT PROUD WHEN
SOMETHING I DID FOR SOMEONE ELSE	I HELPED SOMEONE WITH
SOMETHING I DID FOR MYSELF	I FELT GOOD ABOUT MYSELF WHEN
I HAD A GOOD EXPERIENCE WITH	I LEARNED
I ACCOMPLISHED	I CHALLENGED MYSELF TO

MONDAY:

TUESDAY:

WEDNESDAY:

THURSDAY:

FRIDAY:

SATURDAY:

SUNDAY:

SELF LOVE GROCERY LIST

As you create your grocery list for the week try to incorporate at least one food into each of the following categories to ensure you are taking care of your whole body, mind, and spirit. Plan your trips to the grocery store not just for food to eat but rather food that nourishes you. Under Meal Challenge-- think of a recipe you have been wanting to try, a food you want to cut out or add in to your diet. Do this weekly to see a drastic change in your overall health.

BRAIN FOOD	GUT HEALTH
SKIN AND HAIR CARE	**SLEEP**
HEALTHY INDULGENCES	**HEALTHY MUNCHIES**
HOUSEHOLD	**MEAL CHALLENGE**

YOUR WEEKLY WHY

Use this space to learn, grow and powerfully understand your thoughts and decision-making processes. Do this anytime you need clarity. Write it on a napkin, a back of an envelope, a journal, or anywhere you can write down and work through your thoughts.

The formula is simple.

Think of something during the week that excited you, upset you, stressed you out, made you inexplicably happy, or devastatingly sad. This could be an event, a choice, or even a conversation.

Then ask yourself WHY three times.

Boundaries

Boundaries are an important part of self -care.

Walls are meant to keep people out, boundaries are meant to show people where the door is.

You can come in, but if you violate my space, my values or my trust you must leave.

You can come in, but if you harm me, you must leave.

You can come in, but if your presence becomes uncomfortable or toxic, you must leave.

Take a look at your boundaries. Think of your soul as the bouncer, and the boundary as the door. Which behaviors, words or actions will get someone bounced from your space?

Which boundaries are permanent and non- negotiable? Which boundaries can be discussed and allow for second chances upon discussion and remedy?

MY NEEDS THIS WEEK

Brainstorm your needs this week. Prioritize by number and add to your weekly calendar.

PERSONAL NEEDS:

PROFESSIONAL NEEDS:

SPIRITUAL NEEDS:

PHYSICAL NEEDS

EMOTIONAL NEEDS

PSYCHOLOGICAL NEEDS

IM POSSIBLE SELF WEEKLY SELF CARE PLAN

	MONDAY	TUESDAY	WEDNESDAY	THURSDAY	FRIDAY
PERSONAL					
PROFESSIONAL					
SPIRITUAL					
EMOTIONAL					
PHYSICAL					
PHYSICAL					

Reminders are personal mantras to be used in times of stress, decision-making, or in moments of gratitude and joy. Write your reminder for the week.

Support: Who or what will support you this week in your Self-Care goals.

REMINDERS	SUPPORT

Challenge:

For 24 hours, before making any choices, ask yourself: Is this supporting the person I want to become?"

When the 24 hours have passed come back to this page and write down some of the things that may have pulled you in the wrong direction. Write down how you kept yourself on track. What needs did you fulfill by only making choices that supported your future and future self?

WEEKEND SELF CARE PLAN

PERSONAL	
PROFESSIONAL	
SPIRITUAL	
EMOTIONAL	
PHYSICAL	
PSYCHOLOGICAL	

WEEKLY SELF ESTEEM CHECK IN

Choose 1 of the following prompts to respond to for each day of the week

SOMETHING I DID WELL WAS	I FELT PROUD WHEN
SOMETHING I DID FOR SOMEONE ELSE	I TRIED
SOMETHING I DID FOR MYSELF	I FELT GOOD ABOUT MYSELF WHEN
I HAD A GOOD EXPERIENCE WITH	I LEARNED
I ACCOMPLISHED	I CHALLENGED MYSELF TO

MONDAY:

TUESDAY:

WEDNESDAY:

THURSDAY:

FRIDAY:

SATURDAY:

SUNDAY:

SELF LOVE GROCERY LIST

As you create your grocery list for the week try to incorporate at least one food into each of the following categories to ensure you are taking care of your whole body, mind, and spirit. Plan your trips to the grocery store not just for food to eat but rather food that nourishes you. Under Meal Challenge-- think of a recipe you have been wanting to try, a food you want to cut out or add in to your diet. Do this weekly to see a drastic change in your overall health.

BRAIN FOOD	GUT HEALTH
SKIN AND HAIR CARE	SLEEP
HEALTHY INDULGENCES	HEALTHY MUNCHIES
HOUSEHOLD	MEAL CHALLENGE

YOUR WEEKLY WHY

Use this space to learn, grow and powerfully understand your thoughts and decision-making processes. Do this anytime you need clarity. Write it on a napkin, a back of an envelope, a journal, or anywhere you can write down and work through your thoughts.

The formula is simple.

Think of something during the week that excited you, upset you, stressed you out, made you inexplicably happy, or devastatingly sad. This could be an event, a choice, or even a conversation.

Then ask yourself WHY three times.

LIBERATION LETTER

Use this template to write a letter to someone or something you must release in order to move forward. This letter is meant for you to acknowledge the people, habits or activities that are no longer serving you. Use this template once a month to allow for optimal growth. Use this page or ideally a separate sheet of paper to allow for thoughtful responses.

Dear,

I am choosing to say goodbye because

You should know saying goodbye makes me feel

Since you have been in my life, I have grown by

You have showed me

Because of you a value I have now is

When I say goodbye to you I will no longer

Sincerely,

HELLO LETTER

Now that you have said goodbye to someone or something that has been holding you back from taking care of yourself and living abundantly, you must check in with yourself. This step is crucial as it will promote healing, create a plan to truly move forward and aid in closure. Use template once a month to allow for optimal growth. Use this page or ideally a separate sheet of paper to allow for thoughtful responses.

Dear,

I just said goodbye to

Saying goodbye to makes me feel

but I know it is for the best. Some of the reasons I know this is for the best are because

Moving forward will be hard. That is ok. Please allow yourself time to feel

Some things you can do when you feel upset about closing this chapter are

Some people you can talk to are

There will be ups and downs, good days and bad days. That is part of difficult change, and it is normal and OK. On the really hard days a reminder you can use is

On the really great days a reminder you can use is

Here are three things I feel confident I can do to move forward and say goodbye

1.

2.

3.

Lastly, thank you for acknowledging it was time to let go. Thank you for honoring your health and your spirit. You deserve the best life has to offer and I am proud of you for putting yourself first.

Love always,

5 Minute Reflection

Inside Voices

What does my inner voice sound like?

When did I listen to my inner voice?

What did I notice when I listened to my inner voice?

When did I ignore my inner voice?

What did I notice when I ignored my inner voice?

When do I hear my inner voice the most?

How can I make listening to my inner voice a priority?

IDENTIFY TRIGGERS

A trigger is something that sets off alarms in your body. Often when this happens you are transported back to the original trauma that created the trigger.

Triggers are very personal, different things can trigger different people. A person's trigger is often activated through a sense: smell, sound, touch, taste and sight. Understanding your triggers is important in self-care because it will help you manage your responses to stimuli in your life.

Example of a trigger:

Significant other does not respond to a text for more than an hour. This behavior is unusual and triggers fear. The last time a significant other ignored or did not respond to a text it was because he/she was cheating. THIS IS THE TRIGGER.

Now triggered you have several options on how to handle this situation. The trigger has released fear into your body and mind. You may already be beginning to feel sad mourning the relationship you believe is about to end, you may become angry. You may want to send an aggravated text accusing your significant other of cheating because the trigger has made you believe that is what is happening.

Or

You see the trigger; you name the trigger and you step back from it and look at objectively. Other than the unanswered text is there any evidence of infidelity? Have your significant other shown behaviors of loyalty, love and given you a reason to trust? Is your reaction to the unanswered text actually about your significant other or an unhealed wound from a past relationship?

Understanding your triggers and being able to step back and recognize them as a trigger will help you make better choices and allow for more productive communication. This is part of self-care. You are nurturing your emotions by recognizing they have been harmed and you are shielding them from further damage by managing your responses.

On the following page make a list of known triggers. Visit this list as you notice other triggers.

INDENTIFY TRIGGERS

Emotional States: Example: When I get lonely, I feel like all of my friends are abandoning me. I think this is because when I was young, I was left out of a lot of things.

People: Example: I have a hard time being around very wealthy people. It makes me feel inferior. I think this is because I grew up poor.

Places: Example: I hate the parking lot at Macy's. I sat in my car and cried there after a break up once and every time I am back in that lot, I feel sad.

Things: Example: Forehead kisses. Everyone who ever left me kissed me on the forehead before they were gone. If I get kissed on the forehead, I immediately begin to think that person is planning to leave me.

Other: Example: I get triggered by certain songs that remind me of people I don't like.

VACATION MODE

You have likely heard the advice "create a life you do not need to take a vacation from." The idea that vacations are the only time we are allowed to indulge in rest, food, recreation and fun can be harmful. Instead, take a few minutes to brainstorm ways you can bring elements of vacation into your daily life.

Where do I like to vacation the most?

What is it about that place that brings me so much joy?

How can I bring elements of that vacation spot into my daily routine?

What do I like most about being on vacation?

How can I add what I like most about being on vacation to my daily routine?

How do I feel when I am on vacation?

Is there anywhere else I have that same feeling?

TIPS FOR SELF CARE

Professional:	Personal:	Spiritual:
Buh-Bye #Selfcaresunday, Hello #Selfcaremonday Stop putting self -care on hold Monday-Friday. The notion t is acceptable to beat yourself into the ground during the week and recover in a flurry of pampering on Sunday is a dangerous myth. Give yourself love and care every day of the week for better balance and overall wellness.	**Eat for gratitude** Give your body a thank you meal. Take it out or whip up something nourishing and healthy to thank it for supporting you through the journey of life.	**Prayer** Regardless of religious beliefs, take time each day to speak to the universe and acknowledge powers at work in your life.
Physical:	**Emotional:**	**Psychological:**
HUG. Hugging triggers the release of oxytocin, also known as the "love hormone." This amazing feel-good hormone has super powers. Hugs are healthy. hugs increase the levels of oxytocin which strengthen the immune system, lower blood pressure and reduce cortisol "the stress hormone."	**Nope.** Set boundaries. Know that boundaries may grow and change as you grow and change. That is OK.	**Art.** Art has a powerful effect on our moods. Whether you doodle or color, take a painting class or even draw on the sidewalk in chalk, art is essential to keeping your mind happy, healthy and active.

MY NEEDS THIS WEEK

Brainstorm your needs this week. Prioritize by number and add to your weekly calendar.

PERSONAL NEEDS:

PROFESSIONAL NEEDS:

SPIRITUAL NEEDS:

PHYSICAL NEEDS

EMOTIONAL NEEDS

PSYCHOLOGICAL NEEDS

IM POSSIBLE SELF WEEKLY SELF CARE PLAN

	MONDAY	TUESDAY	WEDNESDAY	THURSDAY	FRIDAY
PERSONAL					
PROFESSIONAL					
SPIRITUAL					
EMOTIONAL					
PHYSICAL					
PHYSICAL					

Reminders are personal mantras to be used in times of stress, decision-making, or in moments of gratitude and joy. Write your reminder for the week.

Support: Who or what will support you this week in your Self-Care goals.

REMINDERS	SUPPORT

WEEKEND SELF CARE PLAN

PERSONAL	
PROFESSIONAL	
SPIRITUAL	
EMOTIONAL	
PHYSICAL	
PSYCHOLOGICAL	

WEEKLY SELF ESTEEM CHECK IN

Choose 1 of the following prompts to respond to for each day of the week

SOMETHING I DID WELL WAS	I FELT PROUD WHEN
SOMETHING I DID FOR SOMEONE ELSE	I TRIED
SOMETHING I DID FOR MYSELF	I FELT GOOD ABOUT MYSELF WHEN
I HAD A GOOD EXPERIENCE WITH	I LEARNED
I ACCOMPLISHED	I CHALLENGED MYSELF TO

MONDAY:

TUESDAY:

WEDNESDAY:

THURSDAY:

FRIDAY:

SATURDAY:

SUNDAY:

Mirror, Mirror

Look in the mirror and list 3 physical attributes that make you feel beautiful. Choose one of those to pamper today.

Example:

Eyes: Take a break from blue lights and screens. Close your eyes and rest. Place cooling tea bags on eyelids.

Legs: Exfoliate with Epsom salt. Give legs a good shave. Take time applying a special lotion.

Lips: Exfoliate, drink more water to hydrate, try a new lip balm.

Skin: Use aloe from an aloe leaf to hydrate and heal skin. Simply place leaf in fridge, cut off small portion, cut off spikes on either side, filet open and rub on skin. Aloe has a host of healing properties and the cooling sensation will tighten pores and reduce inflammation.

SELF LOVE GROCERY LIST

As you create your grocery list for the week try to incorporate at least one food into each of the following categories to ensure you are taking care of your whole body, mind, and spirit. Plan your trips to the grocery store not just for food to eat but rather food that nourishes you. Under Meal Challenge-- think of a recipe you have been wanting to try, a food you want to cut out or add in to your diet. Do this weekly to see a drastic change in your overall health.

BRAIN FOOD	GUT HEALTH
SKIN AND HAIR CARE	SLEEP
HEALTHY INDULGENCES	HEALTHY MUNCHIES
HOUSEHOLD	MEAL CHALLENGE

<u>YOUR WEEKLY WHY</u>

Use this space to learn, grow and powerfully understand your thoughts and decision-making processes. Do this anytime you need clarity. Write it on a napkin, a back of an envelope, a journal, or anywhere you can write down and work through your thoughts.

The formula is simple.

Think of something during the week that excited you, upset you, stressed you out, made you inexplicably happy, or devastatingly sad. This could be an event, a choice, or even a conversation.

Then ask yourself WHY three times.

MY NEEDS THIS WEEK

Brainstorm your needs this week. Prioritize by number and add to your weekly calendar.

PERSONAL NEEDS:

PROFESSIONAL NEEDS:

SPIRITUAL NEEDS:

PHYSICAL NEEDS

EMOTIONAL NEEDS

PSYCHOLOGICAL NEEDS

IM POSSIBLE SELF WEEKLY SELF CARE PLAN

	MONDAY	TUESDAY	WEDNESDAY	THURSDAY	FRIDAY
PERSONAL					
PROFESSIONAL					
SPIRITUAL					
EMOTIONAL					
PHYSICAL					
PHYSICAL					

Reminders are personal mantras to be used in times of stress, decision-making, or in moments of gratitude and joy. Write your reminder for the week.

Support: Who or what will support you this week in your Self-Care goals.

REMINDERS	SUPPORT

You can do anything, but not everything.

Remember that.

WEEKEND SELF CARE PLAN

PERSONAL	
PROFESSIONAL	
SPIRITUAL	
EMOTIONAL	
PHYSICAL	
PSYCHOLOGICAL	

WEEKLY SELF ESTEEM CHECK IN

Choose 2 of the following prompts to respond to for each day of the week

SOMETHING I ENJOYED	I FELT PROUD WHEN
SOMETHING I DID FOR SOMEONE ELSE	I TOOK TIME FOR
SOMETHING I DID FOR MYSELF	I FELT GOOD ABOUT MYSELF WHEN
I GAVE BACK TO MY COMMUNITY BY	I LEARNED
I ACCOMPLISHED	I CHALLENGED MYSELF TO

MONDAY:

TUESDAY:

WEDNESDAY:

THURSDAY:

FRIDAY:

SATURDAY:

SUNDAY:

SELF LOVE GROCERY LIST

As you create your grocery list for the week try to incorporate at least one food into each of the following categories to ensure you are taking care of your whole body, mind, and spirit. Plan your trips to the grocery store not just for food to eat but rather food that nourishes you. Under Meal Challenge-- think of a recipe you have been wanting to try, a food you want to cut out or add in to your diet. Do this weekly to see a drastic change in your overall health.

BRAIN FOOD	GUT HEALTH
SKIN AND HAIR CARE	**SLEEP**
HEALTHY INDULGENCES	**HEALTHY MUNCHIES**
HOUSEHOLD	**MEAL CHALLENGE**

YOUR WEEKLY WHY

Use this space to learn, grow and powerfully understand your thoughts and decision-making processes. Do this anytime you need clarity. Write it on a napkin, a back of an envelope, a journal, or anywhere you can write down and work through your thoughts.

The formula is simple.

Think of something during the week that excited you, upset you, stressed you out, made you inexplicably happy, or devastatingly sad. This could be an event, a choice, or even a conversation.

Then ask yourself WHY three times.

MY NEEDS THIS WEEK

Brainstorm your needs this week. Prioritize by number and add to your weekly calendar.

PERSONAL NEEDS:

PROFESSIONAL NEEDS:

SPIRITUAL NEEDS:

PHYSICAL NEEDS

EMOTIONAL NEEDS

PSYCHOLOGICAL NEEDS

IM POSSIBLE SELF WEEKLY SELF CARE PLAN

	MONDAY	TUESDAY	WEDNESDAY	THURSDAY	FRIDAY
PERSONAL					
PROFESSIONAL					
SPIRITUAL					
EMOTIONAL					
PHYSICAL					
PHYSICAL					

Reminders are personal mantras to be used in times of stress, decision-making, or in moments of gratitude and joy. Write your reminder for the week.

Support: Who or what will support you this week in your Self-Care goals.

REMINDERS	SUPPORT

WEEKEND SELF CARE PLAN

PERSONAL	
PROFESSIONAL	
SPIRITUAL	
EMOTIONAL	
PHYSICAL	
PSYCHOLOGICAL	

WEEKLY SELF ESTEEM CHECK IN

Choose 1 of the following prompts to respond to for each day of the week

SOMETHING I DID WELL WAS	I FELT PROUD WHEN
SOMETHING I DID FOR SOMEONE ELSE	I PUSHED MYSELF TO
SOMETHING I LOVE ABOUT MYSELF	I FELT GOOD ABOUT MYSELF WHEN
I AM HAPPY WITH	I LEARNED
I TOOK A CHANCE AND	I CHALLENGED MYSELF TO

MONDAY:

TUESDAY:

WEDNESDAY:

THURSDAY:

FRIDAY:

SATURDAY:

SUNDAY:

SELF LOVE GROCERY LIST

      As you create your grocery list for the week try to incorporate at least one food into each of the following categories to ensure you are taking care of your whole body, mind, and spirit. Plan your trips to the grocery store not just for food to eat but rather food that nourishes you. Under Meal Challenge-- think of a recipe you have been wanting to try, a food you want to cut out or add in to your diet. Do this weekly to see a drastic change in your overall health.

BRAIN FOOD	GUT HEALTH
SKIN AND HAIR CARE	**SLEEP**
HEALTHY INDULGENCES	**HEALTHY MUNCHIES**
HOUSEHOLD	**MEAL CHALLENGE**

If you could feel a certain way every day, what would it be? What is stopping you from feeling that way? Write down one actionable step you can take to begin feeling that way every day.

YOUR WEEKLY WHY

Use this space to learn, grow and powerfully understand your thoughts and decision-making processes. Do this anytime you need clarity. Write it on a napkin, a back of an envelope, a journal, or anywhere you can write down and work through your thoughts.

The formula is simple.

Think of something during the week that excited you, upset you, stressed you out, made you inexplicably happy, or devastatingly sad. This could be an event, a choice, or even a conversation.

Then ask yourself WHY three times.

MY NEEDS THIS WEEK

Brainstorm your needs this week. Prioritize by number and add to your weekly calendar.

PERSONAL NEEDS:

PROFESSIONAL NEEDS:

SPIRITUAL NEEDS:

PHYSICAL NEEDS

EMOTIONAL NEEDS

PSYCHOLOGICAL NEEDS

IM POSSIBLE SELF WEEKLY SELF CARE PLAN

	MONDAY	TUESDAY	WEDNESDAY	THURSDAY	FRIDAY
PERSONAL					
PROFESSIONAL					
SPIRITUAL					
EMOTIONAL					
PHYSICAL					
PHYSICAL					

Reminders are personal mantras to be used in times of stress, decision-making, or in moments of gratitude and joy. Write your reminder for the week.

Support: Who or what will support you this week in your Self-Care goals.

REMINDERS	SUPPORT

WEEKEND SELF CARE PLAN

PERSONAL	
PROFESSIONAL	
SPIRITUAL	
EMOTIONAL	
PHYSICAL	
PSYCHOLOGICAL	

Observations:

Who or what am I feeling connected to? Why? What positive feelings or experiences is this connection adding to my life?

WEEKLY SELF ESTEEM CHECK IN

Choose 1 of the following prompts to respond to for each day of the week

I LISTENED TO MY GUT WHEN	I FELT PROUD WHEN
SOMETHING I DID FOR SOMEONE ELSE	I GAVE LOVE TO
SOMETHING I DID FOR MYSELF	I FELT GOOD ABOUT MYSELF WHEN
I GAVE MYSELF	I LEARNED
I ACCOMPLISHED	I CHALLENGED MYSELF TO

MONDAY:

TUESDAY:

WEDNESDAY:

THURSDAY:

FRIDAY:

SATURDAY:

SUNDAY:

SELF LOVE GROCERY LIST

As you create your grocery list for the week try to incorporate at least one food into each of the following categories to ensure you are taking care of your whole body, mind, and spirit. Plan your trips to the grocery store not just for food to eat but rather food that nourishes you. Under Meal Challenge-- think of a recipe you have been wanting to try, a food you want to cut out or add in to your diet. Do this weekly to see a drastic change in your overall health.

BRAIN FOOD	GUT HEALTH
SKIN AND HAIR CARE	SLEEP
HEALTHY INDULGENCES	HEALTHY MUNCHIES
HOUSEHOLD	MEAL CHALLENGE

YOUR WEEKLY WHY

Use this space to learn, grow and powerfully understand your thoughts and decision-making processes. Do this anytime you need clarity. Write it on a napkin, a back of an envelope, a journal, or anywhere you can write down and work through your thoughts.

The formula is simple.

Think of something during the week that excited you, upset you, stressed you out, made you inexplicably happy, or devastatingly sad. This could be an event, a choice, or even a conversation.

Then ask yourself WHY three times.

LIBERATION LETTER

Use this template to write a letter to someone or something you must release in order to move forward. This letter is meant for you to acknowledge the people, habits or activities that are no longer serving you. Use this template once a month to allow for optimal growth. Use this page or ideally a separate sheet of paper to allow for thoughtful responses.

Dear,

I am choosing to say goodbye because

You should know saying goodbye makes me feel

You taught me to

I believe that I

Because of you I have learned the value of

When I say goodbye to you I will no longer

Sincerely

HELLO LETTER

Now that you have said goodbye to someone or something that has been holding you back from taking care of yourself and living abundantly, you must check in with yourself. This step is crucial as it will promote healing, create a plan to truly move forward and aid in closure. Use template once a month to allow for optimal growth. Use this page or ideally a separate sheet of paper or blank sheets in back of planner to allow for thoughtful responses.

Dear,

I just said goodbye to

Saying goodbye to makes me feel

but I know it is for the best. Some of the reasons I know this is for the best are because

Moving forward will be hard. That is ok. Please allow yourself time to feel

Some things you can do when you feel upset about closing this chapter are

Some people you can talk to are

There will be ups and downs, good days and bad days. That is part of difficult change, and it is normal and OK. On the really hard days a reminder you can use is

On the really great days a reminder you can use is

Here are three things I feel confident I can do to move forward and say goodbye

1.

2.

3.

Lastly, thank you for acknowledging it was time to let go. Thank you for honoring your health and your spirit. You deserve the best life has to offer and I am proud of you for putting yourself first.

Love always,

FORWARD AND BACK

Being aware of how our past has shaped our present, and in turn, will shape our future is a big part of self-care. If we better understand how we got here we can better navigate the path to where we want to go. In this activity you will be looking at past and future needs.

In the past	Going forward
I was...	I am...
I needed...	I need...
I didn't have...	I have...
I believed....	I believe...

5 Minute Reflection

Affirmations

Write down 4 affirmations you can tell yourself. Use these affirmations in seasons of stress and uncertainty. Or use these affirmations in seasons of happiness and gratitude.

1.

2.

3.

4.

TIPS FOR SELF CARE

Professional:	Personal:	Spiritual:
Challenge yourself. Successful people challenge themselves daily. Whether the challenge is big or small they are the key to unlocking your potential.	**Help Someone.** When you feel helpless, help another. This shifts your energy away from wallowing in self - pity to being of service which will only uplift your spirits.	**Dream Journal** Keep a dream journal by your bed and write down your dreams as you remember them. Often our subconscious is trying to tell us something even in the strangest dreams.
Physical: Get a massage.	**Emotional:** **JOMO.** Find joy in missing out. You do not need to be a part of everything to matter. Your worth is not defined by your social calendar.	**Psychological:** **Vitamin D.** Get outside and get some sunshine on your skin (with SPF)

"There is no such thing as "perfect timing." Done is better than perfect. No one will ever see your potential and what you have to offer if you never have the courage to put it out there."

-Christy Shaterian

MY NEEDS THIS WEEK

Brainstorm your needs this week. Prioritize by number and add to your weekly calendar.

PERSONAL NEEDS:

PROFESSIONAL NEEDS:

SPIRITUAL NEEDS:

PHYSICAL NEEDS

EMOTIONAL NEEDS

PSYCHOLOGICAL NEEDS

IM POSSIBLE SELF WEEKLY SELF CARE PLAN

	MONDAY	TUESDAY	WEDNESDAY	THURSDAY	FRIDAY
PERSONAL					
PROFESSIONAL					
SPIRITUAL					
EMOTIONAL					
PHYSICAL					
PHYSICAL					

Reminders are personal mantras to be used in times of stress, decision-making, or in moments of gratitude and joy. Write your reminder for the week.

Support: Who or what will support you this week in your Self-Care goals.

REMINDERS	SUPPORT

WEEKEND SELF CARE PLAN

PERSONAL	
PROFESSIONAL	
SPIRITUAL	
EMOTIONAL	
PHYSICAL	
PSYCHOLOGICAL	

WEEKLY SELF ESTEEM CHECK IN

Choose 2 of the following prompts to respond to for each day of the week

SOMETHING I DID WELL WAS	I FELT PROUD WHEN
A CHOICE I MADE FOR MYSELF WAS	I SAID YES TO
SOMETHING I DID FOR MYSELF	I FELT GOOD ABOUT MYSELF WHEN
I HAD A GOOD EXPERIENCE WITH	I SET BOUNDARIES AROUND
I ACCOMPLISHED	I CHALLENGED MYSELF TO

MONDAY:

TUESDAY:

WEDNESDAY:

THURSDAY:

FRIDAY:

SATURDAY:

SUNDAY:

Pay it forward

Think of something you have learned, something that has helped you grow and brought joy to your life. How can you pay it forward? Who do you know that could use it right now?

SELF LOVE GROCERY LIST

As you create your grocery list for the week try to incorporate at least one food into each of the following categories to ensure you are taking care of your whole body, mind, and spirit. Plan your trips to the grocery store not just for food to eat but rather food that nourishes you. Under Meal Challenge-- think of a recipe you have been wanting to try, a food you want to cut out or add in to your diet. Do this weekly to see a drastic change in your overall health.

BRAIN FOOD	GUT HEALTH
SKIN AND HAIR CARE	SLEEP
HEALTHY INDULGENCES	HEALTHY MUNCHIES
HOUSEHOLD	MEAL CHALLENGE

Pickled Onions!

Red onions are rich in folate, also known as Vitamin B9. B9 is an essential nutrient for optimal health and overall wellness. Pickled red onions contain many other vitamins and minerals such as calcium, potassium, magnesium, and Vitamin C.

Adding pickled red onions into your diet can also help improve the immune, nervous, and digestive systems of your body.

Pickled red onions contain high amounts of probiotics or digestive enzymes. Maintaining a healthy gut flora can aid your digestion (buh-Bye bloat and weird tummy issues) and overall energy levels. Fermented foods can also lead to improving skin disorders such as acne that can be traced back to the gut.

How to make pickled onions? EASY!

- Thinly slice an onion
- Place in a mason jar
- Whisk together water, ¾ cup white vinegar, ¼ cup white granulated sugar, salt & pepper over medium high heat until boiling.
- Pour liquid over onions
- Close lid, refrigerate at least 24 hours

Try on tacos, salads, or omelets!

YOUR WEEKLY WHY

Use this space to learn, grow and powerfully understand your thoughts and decision-making processes. Do this anytime you need clarity. Write it on a napkin, a back of an envelope, a journal, or anywhere you can write down and work through your thoughts.

The formula is simple.

Think of something during the week that excited you, upset you, stressed you out, made you inexplicably happy, or devastatingly sad. This could be an event, a choice, or even a conversation.

Then ask yourself WHY three times.

MY NEEDS THIS WEEK

Brainstorm your needs this week. Prioritize by number and add to your weekly calendar.

PERSONAL NEEDS:

PROFESSIONAL NEEDS:

SPIRITUAL NEEDS:

PHYSICAL NEEDS

EMOTIONAL NEEDS

PSYCHOLOGICAL NEEDS

IM POSSIBLE SELF WEEKLY SELF CARE PLAN

	MONDAY	TUESDAY	WEDNESDAY	THURSDAY	FRIDAY
PERSONAL					
PROFESSIONAL					
SPIRITUAL					
EMOTIONAL					
PHYSICAL					
PHYSICAL					

Reminders are personal mantras to be used in times of stress, decision-making, or in moments of gratitude and joy. Write your reminder for the week.

Support: Who or what will support you this week in your Self-Care goals.

REMINDERS	SUPPORT

WEEKEND SELF CARE PLAN

PERSONAL	
PROFESSIONAL	
SPIRITUAL	
EMOTIONAL	
PHYSICAL	
PSYCHOLOGICAL	

WEEKLY SELF ESTEEM CHECK IN

Choose 1 of the following prompts to respond to for each day of the week

I APPLIED MY VALUE OF	I FELT PROUD WHEN
SOMETHING I DID FOR SOMEONE ELSE	I FORGAVE
SOMETHING I DID FOR MYSELF	I FELT GOOD ABOUT MYSELF WHEN
I HAD A GOOD EXPERIENCE WITH	I LET GO OF
I ACCOMPLISHED	I CHALLENGED MYSELF TO

MONDAY:

TUESDAY:

WEDNESDAY:

THURSDAY:

FRIDAY:

SATURDAY:

SUNDAY:

SELF LOVE GROCERY LIST

As you create your grocery list for the week try to incorporate at least one food into each of the following categories to ensure you are taking care of your whole body, mind, and spirit. Plan your trips to the grocery store not just for food to eat but rather food that nourishes you. Under Meal Challenge-- think of a recipe you have been wanting to try, a food you want to cut out or add in to your diet. Do this weekly to see a drastic change in your overall health.

BRAIN FOOD	GUT HEALTH
SKIN AND HAIR CARE	**SLEEP**
HEALTHY INDULGENCES	**HEALTHY MUNCHIES**
HOUSEHOLD	**MEAL CHALLENGE**

3 Daily reminders:

I am capable of great things

I am prepared to succeed

I am always learning and THAT is my superpower

How will I recharge this week?

<u>YOUR WEEKLY WHY</u>

Use this space to learn, grow and powerfully understand your thoughts and decision-making processes. Do this anytime you need clarity. Write it on a napkin, a back of an envelope, a journal, or anywhere you can write down and work through your thoughts.

The formula is simple.

Think of something during the week that excited you, upset you, stressed you out, made you inexplicably happy, or devastatingly sad. This could be an event, a choice, or even a conversation.

Then ask yourself WHY three times.

MY NEEDS THIS WEEK

Brainstorm your needs this week. Prioritize by number and add to your weekly calendar.

PERSONAL NEEDS:

PROFESSIONAL NEEDS:

SPIRITUAL NEEDS:

PHYSICAL NEEDS

EMOTIONAL NEEDS

PSYCHOLOGICAL NEEDS

IM POSSIBLE SELF WEEKLY SELF CARE PLAN

	MONDAY	TUESDAY	WEDNESDAY	THURSDAY	FRIDAY
PERSONAL					
PROFESSIONAL					
SPIRITUAL					
EMOTIONAL					
PHYSICAL					
PHYSICAL					

Reminders are personal mantras to be used in times of stress, decision-making, or in moments of gratitude and joy. Write your reminder for the week.

Support: Who or what will support you this week in your Self-Care goals.

REMINDERS	SUPPORT

WEEKEND SELF CARE PLAN

PERSONAL	
PROFESSIONAL	
SPIRITUAL	
EMOTIONAL	
PHYSICAL	
PSYCHOLOGICAL	

WEEKLY SELF ESTEEM CHECK IN

Choose 1 of the following prompts to respond to for each day of the week

SOMETHING I MADE PROGRESS ON	I FELT PROUD WHEN
SOMETHING I DID FOR SOMEONE ELSE	I TRIED A NEW
SOMETHING I DID FOR MYSELF	I FELT GOOD ABOUT MYSELF WHEN
I GAVE HOPE TO	I TRUSTED
I ACCOMPLISHED	I CHALLENGED MYSELF TO

MONDAY:

TUESDAY:

WEDNESDAY:

THURSDAY:

FRIDAY:

SATURDAY:

SUNDAY:

SELF LOVE GROCERY LIST

As you create your grocery list for the week try to incorporate at least one food into each of the following categories to ensure you are taking care of your whole body, mind, and spirit. Plan your trips to the grocery store not just for food to eat but rather food that nourishes you. Under Meal Challenge-- think of a recipe you have been wanting to try, a food you want to cut out or add in to your diet. Do this weekly to see a drastic change in your overall health.

BRAIN FOOD	GUT HEALTH
SKIN AND HAIR CARE	**SLEEP**
HEALTHY INDULGENCES	**HEALTHY MUNCHIES**
HOUSEHOLD	**MEAL CHALLENGE**

YOUR WEEKLY WHY

Use this space to learn, grow and powerfully understand your thoughts and decision-making processes. Do this anytime you need clarity. Write it on a napkin, a back of an envelope, a journal, or anywhere you can write down and work through your thoughts.

The formula is simple.

Think of something during the week that excited you, upset you, stressed you out, made you inexplicably happy, or devastatingly sad. This could be an event, a choice, or even a conversation.

Then ask yourself WHY three times.

MY NEEDS THIS WEEK

Brainstorm your needs this week. Prioritize by number and add to your weekly calendar.

PERSONAL NEEDS:

PROFESSIONAL NEEDS:

SPIRITUAL NEEDS:

PHYSICAL NEEDS

EMOTIONAL NEEDS

PSYCHOLOGICAL NEEDS

IM POSSIBLE SELF WEEKLY SELF CARE PLAN

	MONDAY	TUESDAY	WEDNESDAY	THURSDAY	FRIDAY
PERSONAL					
PROFESSIONAL					
SPIRITUAL					
EMOTIONAL					
PHYSICAL					
PHYSICAL					

Reminders are personal mantras to be used in times of stress, decision-making, or in moments of gratitude and joy. Write your reminder for the week.

Support: Who or what will support you this week in your Self-Care goals.

REMINDERS	SUPPORT

WEEKEND SELF CARE PLAN

PERSONAL	
PROFESSIONAL	
SPIRITUAL	
EMOTIONAL	
PHYSICAL	
PSYCHOLOGICAL	

WEEKLY SELF ESTEEM CHECK IN

Choose 1 of the following prompts to respond to for each day of the week

I BELIEVED IN MYSELF WHEN	I FELT PROUD WHEN
SOMETHING I DID FOR SOMEONE ELSE	AN ACT OF KINDNESS I GAVE WAS
SOMETHING I DID FOR MYSELF	I FELT GOOD ABOUT MYSELF WHEN
I TOOK A CHANCE BY	I EXPLORED
I ACCOMPLISHED	I CHALLENGED MYSELF TO

MONDAY:

TUESDAY:

WEDNESDAY:

THURSDAY:

FRIDAY:

SATURDAY:

SUNDAY:

SELF LOVE GROCERY LIST

As you create your grocery list for the week try to incorporate at least one food into each of the following categories to ensure you are taking care of your whole body, mind, and spirit. Plan your trips to the grocery store not just for food to eat but rather food that nourishes you. Under Meal Challenge-- think of a recipe you have been wanting to try, a food you want to cut out or add in to your diet. Do this weekly to see a drastic change in your overall health.

BRAIN FOOD	GUT HEALTH
SKIN AND HAIR CARE	**SLEEP**
HEALTHY INDULGENCES	**HEALTHY MUNCHIES**
HOUSEHOLD	**MEAL CHALLENGE**

What is not wrong?

We spend a lot of time during seasons of change looking at what isn't working and we often overlook what IS working.

So, hey, what's NOT wrong?

YOUR WEEKLY WHY

Use this space to learn, grow and powerfully understand your thoughts and decision-making processes. Do this anytime you need clarity. Write it on a napkin, a back of an envelope, a journal, or anywhere you can write down and work through your thoughts.

The formula is simple.

Think of something during the week that excited you, upset you, stressed you out, made you inexplicably happy, or devastatingly sad. This could be an event, a choice, or even a conversation.

Then ask yourself WHY three times.

LIBERATION LETTER

Use this template to write a letter to someone or something you must release in order to move forward. This letter is meant for you to acknowledge the people, habits or activities that are no longer serving you. Use this template once a month to allow for optimal growth. Use this page or ideally a separate sheet of paper to allow for thoughtful responses.

Dear,

I am choosing to say goodbye because

You should know saying goodbye makes me feel

I would like to thank you for showing me

You gave me

I now know that I

When I say goodbye to you I will no longer

Sincerely,

HELLO LETTER

Now that you have said goodbye to someone or something that has been holding you back from taking care of yourself and living abundantly, you must check in with yourself. This step is crucial as it will promote healing, create a plan to truly move forward and aid in closure. Use template once a month to allow for optimal growth. Use this page or ideally a separate sheet of paper or blank sheets in back of planner to allow for thoughtful responses.

Dear,

I just said goodbye to

Saying goodbye to makes me feel

but I know it is for the best. Some of the reasons I know this is for the best are because

Moving forward will be hard. That is ok. Please allow yourself time to feel

Some things you can do when you feel upset about closing this chapter are

Some people you can talk to are

There will be ups and downs, good days and bad days. That is part of difficult change, and it is normal and OK. On the really hard days a reminder you can use is

On the really great days a reminder you can use is

Here are three things I feel confident I can do to move forward and say goodbye

1.

2.

3.

Lastly, thank you for acknowledging it was time to let go. Thank you for honoring your health and your spirit. You deserve the best life has to offer and I am proud of you for putting yourself first.

Love always,

5 Minute Reflection

Hey Batter, Batter

What is your "up to bat" song? When a baseball player gets up to bat, they play a song that hypes up the crowd and themselves. What is your hype up song and why?

Who Can I Call When...?

It is important to know who your lifelines are. Examine your support system and answer the following prompts.

Who can I call when I feel lonely and why?

Who can I call when I want to share a big win and why?

Who can I call when I need someone to talk to and why?

Who can I call when I want to be my truest self without judgement and why?

Who can I call to support me in my self-care journey and why?

TIPS FOR SELF CARE

Professional:	Personal:	Spiritual:
Practice being mindful. Being mindful is being self-aware of what is going on around you but more importantly what is going on INSIDE OF YOU. Being mindful of your needs will help boost your ability to make wise professional choices and to control your emotions in times of stress.	**Hobby** Pick up a hobby you have always wanted to learn. Learning something new has been proven to increase your self-esteem. As you master your new skill you will soon realize you have even more to offer than you thought possible. You are capable of all things.	**Read More.** Feed your mind with information.
Physical:	**Emotional:**	**Psychological:**
Epsom Salt Epsom salt is an excellent exfoliant. Pat some on face and body and allow it to absorb into skin for up to 5 minutes. Rinse off in a circular motion to exfoliate skin while receiving benefits of the salt.	**Talk it out** Everyone needs a friend they can talk to and vent while not being held accountable for what is said in the moment. Find, cherish and spend time with the people who allow you to express our emotions as you feel them.	**Set a short -term goal.** Setting a short-term goal will boost your confidence and set you up for great success with long term goals. Essentially you are reminding yourself that you are capable!

"Dig deep within yourself to mine your diamonds, then go out and share them with the world."

-Katherine Alexander

MY NEEDS THIS WEEK

Brainstorm your needs this week. Prioritize by number and add to your weekly calendar.

PERSONAL NEEDS:

PROFESSIONAL NEEDS:

SPIRITUAL NEEDS:

PHYSICAL NEEDS

EMOTIONAL NEEDS

PSYCHOLOGICAL NEEDS

IM POSSIBLE SELF WEEKLY SELF CARE PLAN

	MONDAY	TUESDAY	WEDNESDAY	THURSDAY	FRIDAY
PERSONAL					
PROFESSIONAL					
SPIRITUAL					
EMOTIONAL					
PHYSICAL					
PHYSICAL					

Reminders are personal mantras to be used in times of stress, decision-making, or in moments of gratitude and joy. Write your reminder for the week.

Support: Who or what will support you this week in your Self-Care goals.

REMINDERS	SUPPORT

WEEKEND SELF CARE PLAN

PERSONAL	
PROFESSIONAL	
SPIRITUAL	
EMOTIONAL	
PHYSICAL	
PSYCHOLOGICAL	

WEEKLY SELF ESTEEM CHECK IN

Choose 1 of the following prompts to respond to for each day of the week

I ACHIEVED	I FELT PROUD WHEN
SOMETHING I DID FOR SOMEONE ELSE	I THANKED MYSELF BY
SOMETHING I DID FOR MYSELF	I FELT GOOD ABOUT MYSELF WHEN
I WORKED HARD ON	I LET GO OF
I ACCOMPLISHED	I CHALLENGED MYSELF TO

MONDAY:

TUESDAY:

WEDNESDAY:

THURSDAY:

FRIDAY:

SATURDAY:

SUNDAY:

We often feel tired not because we have done too much, but rather we have done too much of the wrong thing, and too little of what inspires us.

What inspires you? What brings you the ultimate joy? What makes you dream? What sets your soul on fire?

What drains you? What is uninspiring (besides laundry, duh.) for you?

Make a list of what brings you joy and what is joyless.

Take a good look at the list. What can you add in to your daily life? What can you take out? Or do you see a balance you are comfortable with?

SELF LOVE GROCERY LIST

As you create your grocery list for the week try to incorporate at least one food into each of the following categories to ensure you are taking care of your whole body, mind, and spirit. Plan your trips to the grocery store not just for food to eat but rather food that nourishes you. Under Meal Challenge-- think of a recipe you have been wanting to try, a food you want to cut out or add in to your diet. Do this weekly to see a drastic change in your overall health.

BRAIN FOOD	GUT HEALTH
SKIN AND HAIR CARE	SLEEP
HEALTHY INDULGENCES	HEALTHY MUNCHIES
HOUSEHOLD	MEAL CHALLENGE

FOOD FOR THOUGHT:

Ask yourself "Will I be happy if I am in the same spot 12 months from now?"

Write down the reasons you don't believe you will be happy in the same spot 12 months from now and some steps towards change.

Write down the reasons you believe you will be happy in 12 months even if you are in the same spot. Do not lose sight of what is good right now about your life and what is good about who you are today.

<u>YOUR WEEKLY WHY</u>

Use this space to learn, grow and powerfully understand your thoughts and decision-making processes. Do this anytime you need clarity. Write it on a napkin, a back of an envelope, a journal, or anywhere you can write down and work through your thoughts.

The formula is simple.

Think of something during the week that excited you, upset you, stressed you out, made you inexplicably happy, or devastatingly sad. This could be an event, a choice, or even a conversation.

Then ask yourself WHY three times.

MY NEEDS THIS WEEK

Brainstorm your needs this week. Prioritize by number and add to your weekly calendar.

PERSONAL NEEDS:

PROFESSIONAL NEEDS:

SPIRITUAL NEEDS:

PHYSICAL NEEDS

EMOTIONAL NEEDS

PSYCHOLOGICAL NEEDS

IM POSSIBLE SELF WEEKLY SELF CARE PLAN

	MONDAY	TUESDAY	WEDNESDAY	THURSDAY	FRIDAY
PERSONAL					
PROFESSIONAL					
SPIRITUAL					
EMOTIONAL					
PHYSICAL					
PHYSICAL					

Reminders are personal mantras to be used in times of stress, decision-making, or in moments of gratitude and joy. Write your reminder for the week.

Support: Who or what will support you this week in your Self-Care goals.

REMINDERS	SUPPORT

WEEKEND SELF CARE PLAN

PERSONAL	
PROFESSIONAL	
SPIRITUAL	
EMOTIONAL	
PHYSICAL	
PSYCHOLOGICAL	

WEEKLY SELF ESTEEM CHECK IN

Choose 1 of the following prompts to respond to for each day of the week

I LOVE (BLANK) ABOUT MYSELF	I FELT GREAT WHEN I
SOMETHING I DID FOR SOMEONE ELSE	I TRIED
SOMETHING I DID FOR MYSELF	I KNOW I AM CAPABLE BECAUSE
I HAD A GOOD EXPERIENCE WITH	I LEARNED
I ACCOMPLISHED	I CHALLENGED MYSELF TO

MONDAY:

TUESDAY:

WEDNESDAY:

THURSDAY:

FRIDAY:

SATURDAY:

SUNDAY:

SELF LOVE GROCERY LIST

As you create your grocery list for the week try to incorporate at least one food into each of the following categories to ensure you are taking care of your whole body, mind, and spirit. Plan your trips to the grocery store not just for food to eat but rather food that nourishes you. Under Meal Challenge-- think of a recipe you have been wanting to try, a food you want to cut out or add in to your diet. Do this weekly to see a drastic change in your overall health.

BRAIN FOOD	GUT HEALTH
SKIN AND HAIR CARE	**SLEEP**
HEALTHY INDULGENCES	**HEALTHY MUNCHIES**
HOUSEHOLD	**MEAL CHALLENGE**

Organize

Reduce stress in the home by creating a space for things you use regularly, or lose regularly.

Buy baskets at the Dollar Store and labels. Place those items in the baskets and label.

You will never have to lose your mind again searching for band aids, batteries or extra hair ties.

Simple organization can reduce stressful situations and feelings of chaos in the home making it easier to focus on your wellbeing.

YOUR WEEKLY WHY

Use this space to learn, grow and powerfully understand your thoughts and decision-making processes. Do this anytime you need clarity. Write it on a napkin, a back of an envelope, a journal, or anywhere you can write down and work through your thoughts.

The formula is simple.

Think of something during the week that excited you, upset you, stressed you out, made you inexplicably happy, or devastatingly sad. This could be an event, a choice, or even a conversation.

Then ask yourself WHY three times.

MY NEEDS THIS WEEK

Brainstorm your needs this week. Prioritize by number and add to your weekly calendar.

PERSONAL NEEDS:

PROFESSIONAL NEEDS:

SPIRITUAL NEEDS:

PHYSICAL NEEDS

EMOTIONAL NEEDS

PSYCHOLOGICAL NEEDS

IM POSSIBLE SELF WEEKLY SELF CARE PLAN

	MONDAY	TUESDAY	WEDNESDAY	THURSDAY	FRIDAY
PERSONAL					
PROFESSIONAL					
SPIRITUAL					
EMOTIONAL					
PHYSICAL					
PHYSICAL					

Reminders are personal mantras to be used in times of stress, decision-making, or in moments of gratitude and joy. Write your reminder for the week.

Support: Who or what will support you this week in your Self-Care goals.

REMINDERS	SUPPORT

WEEKEND SELF CARE PLAN

PERSONAL	
PROFESSIONAL	
SPIRITUAL	
EMOTIONAL	
PHYSICAL	
PSYCHOLOGICAL	

WEEKLY SELF ESTEEM CHECK IN

Choose 1 of the following prompts to respond to for each day of the week

I ENJOYED	I FELT PROUD WHEN
SOMETHING I DID FOR SOMEONE ELSE	I SAID YES TO
SOMETHING I DID FOR MYSELF	I FELT GOOD ABOUT MYSELF WHEN
I ADVOCATED FOR	I LEARNED ABOUT
I SAID NO TO	I CHALLENGED MYSELF TO

MONDAY:

TUESDAY:

WEDNESDAY:

THURSDAY:

FRIDAY:

SATURDAY:

SUNDAY:

Doodle

Doodle your favorite memory. What about this memory makes it your favorite?

SELF LOVE GROCERY LIST

As you create your grocery list for the week try to incorporate at least one food into each of the following categories to ensure you are taking care of your whole body, mind, and spirit. Plan your trips to the grocery store not just for food to eat but rather food that nourishes you. Under Meal Challenge-- think of a recipe you have been wanting to try, a food you want to cut out or add in to your diet. Do this weekly to see a drastic change in your overall health.

BRAIN FOOD	GUT HEALTH
SKIN AND HAIR CARE	SLEEP
HEALTHY INDULGENCES	HEALTHY MUNCHIES
HOUSEHOLD	MEAL CHALLENGE

Selfie Challenge:

Take a selfie. You do not need to post it. Choose 3 things you like about the way you look.

YOUR WEEKLY WHY

Use this space to learn, grow and powerfully understand your thoughts and decision-making processes. Do this anytime you need clarity. Write it on a napkin, a back of an envelope, a journal, or anywhere you can write down and work through your thoughts.

The formula is simple.

Think of something during the week that excited you, upset you, stressed you out, made you inexplicably happy, or devastatingly sad. This could be an event, a choice, or even a conversation.

Then ask yourself WHY three times.

MY NEEDS THIS WEEK

Brainstorm your needs this week. Prioritize by number and add to your weekly calendar.

PERSONAL NEEDS:

PROFESSIONAL NEEDS:

SPIRITUAL NEEDS:

PHYSICAL NEEDS

EMOTIONAL NEEDS

PSYCHOLOGICAL NEEDS

IM POSSIBLE SELF WEEKLY SELF CARE PLAN

	MONDAY	TUESDAY	WEDNESDAY	THURSDAY	FRIDAY
PERSONAL					
PROFESSIONAL					
SPIRITUAL					
EMOTIONAL					
PHYSICAL					
PHYSICAL					

Reminders are personal mantras to be used in times of stress, decision-making, or in moments of gratitude and joy. Write your reminder for the week.

Support: Who or what will support you this week in your Self-Care goals.

REMINDERS	SUPPORT

WEEKEND SELF CARE PLAN

PERSONAL	
PROFESSIONAL	
SPIRITUAL	
EMOTIONAL	
PHYSICAL	
PSYCHOLOGICAL	

WEEKLY SELF ESTEEM CHECK IN

Choose 1 of the following prompts to respond to for each day of the week

SOMETHING I DID WELL WAS	I FELT PROUD WHEN
SOMETHING I DID FOR SOMEONE ELSE	I TRIED
SOMETHING I DID FOR MYSELF	I FELT GOOD ABOUT MYSELF WHEN
I HAD A GOOD EXPERIENCE WITH	I LEARNED
I ACCOMPLISHED	I CHALLENGED MYSELF TO

MONDAY:

TUESDAY:

WEDNESDAY:

THURSDAY:

FRIDAY:

SATURDAY:

SUNDAY:

SELF LOVE GROCERY LIST

As you create your grocery list for the week try to incorporate at least one food into each of the following categories to ensure you are taking care of your whole body, mind, and spirit. Plan your trips to the grocery store not just for food to eat but rather food that nourishes you. Under Meal Challenge-- think of a recipe you have been wanting to try, a food you want to cut out or add in to your diet. Do this weekly to see a drastic change in your overall health.

BRAIN FOOD	GUT HEALTH
SKIN AND HAIR CARE	**SLEEP**
HEALTHY INDULGENCES	**HEALTHY MUNCHIES**
HOUSEHOLD	**MEAL CHALLENGE**

Vitamin B: The Anxiety Slayer

Vitamin B1 is important for balancing blood sugar levels which can play a significant role in anxiety levels. Ever forget to eat and then find yourself panicky, having severe mood swings (even falling into deep depressive states)? A likely culprit is blood sugar!

Vitamin B3 plays a critical role in the synthesis of serotonin and has been shown to help with anxiety.

Vitamin B5 supports the adrenal glands which reduces stress and anxiety levels.

Vitamin B9 (also known as folate or folic acid) and vitamin B12 are vital in balancing out depressive moods.

Where to find Vitamin B?

Fish, tofu, red meat, cottage cheese, eggs and avocados

YOUR WEEKLY WHY

Use this space to learn, grow and powerfully understand your thoughts and decision-making processes. Do this anytime you need clarity. Write it on a napkin, a back of an envelope, a journal, or anywhere you can write down and work through your thoughts.

The formula is simple.

Think of something during the week that excited you, upset you, stressed you out, made you inexplicably happy, or devastatingly sad. This could be an event, a choice, or even a conversation.

Then ask yourself WHY three times.

LIBERATION LETTER

Use this template to write a letter to someone or something you must release in order to move forward. This letter is meant for you to acknowledge the people, habits or activities that are no longer serving you. Use this template once a month to allow for optimal growth. Use this page or ideally a separate sheet of paper to allow for thoughtful responses.

Dear,

I am choosing to say goodbye because

You should know saying goodbye makes me feel

Your presence in my life showed me

A value I learned was

My inner voice is telling me

When I say goodbye to you I will no longer

Sincerely,

HELLO LETTER

Now that you have said goodbye to someone or something that has been holding you back from taking care of yourself and living abundantly, you must check in with yourself. This step is crucial as it will promote healing, create a plan to truly move forward and aid in closure. Use template once a month to allow for optimal growth. Use this page or ideally a separate sheet of paper or blank sheets in back of planner to allow for thoughtful responses.

Dear,

I just said goodbye to

Saying goodbye to makes me feel

but I know it is for the best. Some of the reasons I know this is for the best are because

Moving forward will be hard. That is ok. Please allow yourself time to feel

Some things you can do when you feel upset about closing this chapter are

Some people you can talk to are

There will be ups and downs, good days and bad days. That is part of difficult change, and it is normal and OK. On the really hard days a reminder you can use is

On the really great days a reminder you can use is

Here are three things I feel confident I can do to move forward and say goodbye

1.

2.

3.

Lastly, thank you for acknowledging it was time to let go. Thank you for honoring your health and your spirit. You deserve the best life has to offer and I am proud of you for putting yourself first.

Love always,

5 Minute Reflection

Values

Knowing your values is important in developing a healthy lifestyle. Your values should be the guiding forces behind your actions, your words, choices, and relationships. Take 5 minutes to list your values and note if you are or are not being led by these values.

What is most important to me? How am I making it a priority in my life? In what ways could I make it more of a priority (if possible)

What do I want for my future? What am I doing daily to work towards that future? Are my actions and choices in line with what I value for my future self?

What do I think the world needs? What am I doing to help the world receive that?

What are three things I will not compromise? Have I, or am I compromising those things?

How do I stay true to my values?

CHALLENGING NEGATIVE THOUGHTS

Negative thoughts have the power to affect our mood and our life. It is important to know how to control your negative thoughts so your negative thoughts do not control you.

Next time something happens that triggers a negative narrative in your mind, consider the following questions. If you can recall an instance recently where you felt overpowered by a negative thought, write it out and answer the following prompts.

What happened that prompted the negative thought?

What negative thought did I form when this happened?

Why is what happened affecting you so deeply? (I.e. perhaps a trigger?)

How does what has happened affect the next 24 hours? Will it impact the next 48? Or will your negative thought be the catalyst for a drawn-out situation?

How does what happened affect your quality of life?

How much power are you giving to this negative thought?

Does that negative thought deserve to have power over you?

Is there evidence to disprove your negative thought?

Is there something you can say to yourself when you feel controlled by a negative thought?

Is there something positive you can do, or a place you can go to clear the negative thoughts from your head?

TIPS FOR SELF CARE

Professional	Personal:	Spiritual:
Declutter Tidy up your office space from time to time. Give it a deep clean. Remove anything you no longer need and give your work space room for growth.	**How are you?** Ask a friend or a family member and then ask it again. Showing you genuinely care about HOW someone you love is truly doing will help form deeper personal connections.	**Retreat.** Plan some time away from it all. Maybe camping, or a yoga retreat, visit a wellness center, spend the afternoon at the beach. Retreat from the hustle and be at one with yourself and the spiritual world around you.
Physical:	**Emotional:**	**Psychological:**
Improve gut health There are around 40 trillion bacteria in your body, most of which, are in your intestines and critical to your health. Increase fruit and veggie intake. Many of these are high in fiber and fiber helps to promote the growth of beneficial gut bacteria.	**Essential Oils.** Tree, grasses and herbs tea tree, cedarwood, frankincense, cypress, lemongrass, sage, goldenrod) promote soothing, renewing and grounding feelings, Try lavender for rest and citrus and mint to uplifted.	**Consistency** Create a schedule that works for you and stick to it. Creating consistence in your life helps to relieve some of the symptoms of anxiety. Hey! I know a planner that helps with this!

"Let your brightness shine from within and remember that you are responsible for keeping your internal fire lit. Pursue only what fuels your flame and avoid all that depletes your oxygen."

-Stephanie Wycoff

MY NEEDS THIS WEEK

Brainstorm your needs this week. Prioritize by number and add to your weekly calendar.

PERSONAL NEEDS:

PROFESSIONAL NEEDS:

SPIRITUAL NEEDS:

PHYSICAL NEEDS

EMOTIONAL NEEDS

PSYCHOLOGICAL NEEDS

IM POSSIBLE SELF WEEKLY SELF CARE PLAN

	MONDAY	TUESDAY	WEDNESDAY	THURSDAY	FRIDAY
PERSONAL					
PROFESSIONAL					
SPIRITUAL					
EMOTIONAL					
PHYSICAL					
PHYSICAL					

Reminders are personal mantras to be used in times of stress, decision-making, or in moments of gratitude and joy. Write your reminder for the week.

Support: Who or what will support you this week in your Self-Care goals.

REMINDERS	SUPPORT

WEEKEND SELF CARE PLAN

PERSONAL	
PROFESSIONAL	
SPIRITUAL	
EMOTIONAL	
PHYSICAL	
PSYCHOLOGICAL	

WEEKLY SELF ESTEEM CHECK IN

Choose 2 of the following prompts to respond to for each day of the week

SOMETHING I LIKE ABOUT MYSELF	I FELT PROUD WHEN
SOMETHING I DID FOR SOMEONE ELSE	I WORKED ON
SOMETHING I DID FOR MYSELF	I FELT GOOD ABOUT MYSELF WHEN
I HAD NOTICED THAT I	I LISTENED TO
I ACCOMPLISHED	I CHALLENGED MYSELF TO

MONDAY:

TUESDAY:

WEDNESDAY:

THURSDAY:

FRIDAY:

SATURDAY:

SUNDAY:

SELF LOVE GROCERY LIST

As you create your grocery list for the week try to incorporate at least one food into each of the following categories to ensure you are taking care of your whole body, mind, and spirit. Plan your trips to the grocery store not just for food to eat but rather food that nourishes you. Under Meal Challenge-- think of a recipe you have been wanting to try, a food you want to cut out or add in to your diet. Do this weekly to see a drastic change in your overall health.

BRAIN FOOD	GUT HEALTH
SKIN AND HAIR CARE	**SLEEP**
HEALTHY INDULGENCES	**HEALTHY MUNCHIES**
HOUSEHOLD	**MEAL CHALLENGE**

YOUR WEEKLY WHY

Use this space to learn, grow and powerfully understand your thoughts and decision-making processes. Do this anytime you need clarity. Write it on a napkin, a back of an envelope, a journal, or anywhere you can write down and work through your thoughts.

The formula is simple.

Think of something during the week that excited you, upset you, stressed you out, made you inexplicably happy, or devastatingly sad. This could be an event, a choice, or even a conversation.

Then ask yourself WHY three times.

MY NEEDS THIS WEEK

Brainstorm your needs this week. Prioritize by number and add to your weekly calendar.

PERSONAL NEEDS:

PROFESSIONAL NEEDS:

SPIRITUAL NEEDS:

PHYSICAL NEEDS

EMOTIONAL NEEDS

PSYCHOLOGICAL NEEDS

IM POSSIBLE SELF WEEKLY SELF CARE PLAN

	MONDAY	TUESDAY	WEDNESDAY	THURSDAY	FRIDAY
PERSONAL					
PROFESSIONAL					
SPIRITUAL					
EMOTIONAL					
PHYSICAL					
PHYSICAL					

Reminders are personal mantras to be used in times of stress, decision-making, or in moments of gratitude and joy. Write your reminder for the week.

Support: Who or what will support you this week in your Self-Care goals.

REMINDERS	SUPPORT

WEEKEND SELF CARE PLAN

PERSONAL	
PROFESSIONAL	
SPIRITUAL	
EMOTIONAL	
PHYSICAL	
PSYCHOLOGICAL	

WEEKLY SELF ESTEEM CHECK IN

Choose 3 of the following prompts to respond to for each day of the week

SOMETHING I DID WELL WAS	I FELT PROUD WHEN
SOMETHING I DID FOR SOMEONE ELSE	I TRIED
SOMETHING I DID FOR MYSELF	I FELT GOOD ABOUT MYSELF WHEN
I HAD A GOOD EXPERIENCE WITH	I LEARNED
I ACCOMPLISHED	I CHALLENGED MYSELF TO

MONDAY:

TUESDAY:

WEDNESDAY:

THURSDAY:

FRIDAY:

SATURDAY:

SUNDAY:

SELF LOVE GROCERY LIST

As you create your grocery list for the week try to incorporate at least one food into each of the following categories to ensure you are taking care of your whole body, mind, and spirit. Plan your trips to the grocery store not just for food to eat but rather food that nourishes you. Under Meal Challenge-- think of a recipe you have been wanting to try, a food you want to cut out or add in to your diet. Do this weekly to see a drastic change in your overall health.

BRAIN FOOD	GUT HEALTH
SKIN AND HAIR CARE	SLEEP
HEALTHY INDULGENCES	HEALTHY MUNCHIES
HOUSEHOLD	MEAL CHALLENGE

YOUR WEEKLY WHY

Use this space to learn, grow and powerfully understand your thoughts and decision-making processes. Do this anytime you need clarity. Write it on a napkin, a back of an envelope, a journal, or anywhere you can write down and work through your thoughts.

The formula is simple.

Think of something during the week that excited you, upset you, stressed you out, made you inexplicably happy, or devastatingly sad. This could be an event, a choice, or even a conversation.

Then ask yourself WHY three times.

MY NEEDS THIS WEEK

Brainstorm your needs this week. Prioritize by number and add to your weekly calendar.

PERSONAL NEEDS:

PROFESSIONAL NEEDS:

SPIRITUAL NEEDS:

PHYSICAL NEEDS

EMOTIONAL NEEDS

PSYCHOLOGICAL NEEDS

IM POSSIBLE SELF WEEKLY SELF CARE PLAN

	MONDAY	TUESDAY	WEDNESDAY	THURSDAY	FRIDAY
PERSONAL					
PROFESSIONAL					
SPIRITUAL					
EMOTIONAL					
PHYSICAL					
PHYSICAL					

Reminders are personal mantras to be used in times of stress, decision-making, or in moments of gratitude and joy. Write your reminder for the week.

Support: Who or what will support you this week in your Self-Care goals.

REMINDERS	SUPPORT

WEEKEND SELF CARE PLAN

PERSONAL	
PROFESSIONAL	
SPIRITUAL	
EMOTIONAL	
PHYSICAL	
PSYCHOLOGICAL	

Doodles:

Doodle three things that make you happiest

WEEKLY SELF ESTEEM CHECK IN

Choose 1 of the following prompts to respond to for each day of the week

SOMETHING I DID WELL WAS	I FELT PROUD WHEN
SOMETHING I DID FOR SOMEONE ELSE	I LOOKED AFTER MYSELF BY
SOMETHING I EXPLORED	I FELT GOOD ABOUT MYSELF WHEN
I TOOK A CHANCE AND	I LEARNED
I MEDITATED ON	I CHALLENGED MYSELF TO

MONDAY:

TUESDAY:

WEDNESDAY:

THURSDAY:

FRIDAY:

SATURDAY:

SUNDAY:

What does my perfect day look like? Is there one element of that day I can start incorporating into my routine today?

SELF LOVE GROCERY LIST

As you create your grocery list for the week try to incorporate at least one food into each of the following categories to ensure you are taking care of your whole body, mind, and spirit. Plan your trips to the grocery store not just for food to eat but rather food that nourishes you. Under Meal Challenge-- think of a recipe you have been wanting to try, a food you want to cut out or add in to your diet. Do this weekly to see a drastic change in your overall health.

BRAIN FOOD	GUT HEALTH
SKIN AND HAIR CARE	**SLEEP**
HEALTHY INDULGENCES	**HEALTHY MUNCHIES**
HOUSEHOLD	**MEAL CHALLENGE**

Who inspires me to cook? What is it about that person's food I like the most? What does that tell me about my food preferences?

YOUR WEEKLY WHY

Use this space to learn, grow and powerfully understand your thoughts and decision-making processes. Do this anytime you need clarity. Write it on a napkin, a back of an envelope, a journal, or anywhere you can write down and work through your thoughts.

The formula is simple.

Think of something during the week that excited you, upset you, stressed you out, made you inexplicably happy, or devastatingly sad. This could be an event, a choice, or even a conversation.

Then ask yourself WHY three times.

MY NEEDS THIS WEEK

Brainstorm your needs this week. Prioritize by number and add to your weekly calendar.

PERSONAL NEEDS:

PROFESSIONAL NEEDS:

SPIRITUAL NEEDS:

PHYSICAL NEEDS

EMOTIONAL NEEDS

PSYCHOLOGICAL NEEDS

IM POSSIBLE SELF WEEKLY SELF CARE PLAN

	MONDAY	TUESDAY	WEDNESDAY	THURSDAY	FRIDAY
PERSONAL					
PROFESSIONAL					
SPIRITUAL					
EMOTIONAL					
PHYSICAL					
PHYSICAL					

Reminders are personal mantras to be used in times of stress, decision-making, or in moments of gratitude and joy. Write your reminder for the week.

Support: Who or what will support you this week in your Self-Care goals.

REMINDERS	SUPPORT

WEEKEND SELF CARE PLAN

PERSONAL	
PROFESSIONAL	
SPIRITUAL	
EMOTIONAL	
PHYSICAL	
PSYCHOLOGICAL	

WEEKLY SELF ESTEEM CHECK IN

Choose 1 of the following prompts to respond to for each day of the week

SOMETHING I DID FOR THE FIRST TIME	I FELT PROUD WHEN
SOMETHING I DID FOR SOMEONE ELSE	I AM THANKFUL FOR MY
SOMETHING I DID FOR MYSELF	I FELT GOOD ABOUT MYSELF WHEN
I HAD A GOOD EXPERIENCE WITH	I AM HAPPY WITH MY
I ACCOMPLISHED	I CHALLENGED MYSELF TO

MONDAY:

TUESDAY:

WEDNESDAY:

THURSDAY:

FRIDAY:

SATURDAY:

SUNDAY:

SELF LOVE GROCERY LIST

As you create your grocery list for the week try to incorporate at least one food into each of the following categories to ensure you are taking care of your whole body, mind, and spirit. Plan your trips to the grocery store not just for food to eat but rather food that nourishes you. Under Meal Challenge-- think of a recipe you have been wanting to try, a food you want to cut out or add in to your diet. Do this weekly to see a drastic change in your overall health.

BRAIN FOOD	GUT HEALTH
SKIN AND HAIR CARE	SLEEP
HEALTHY INDULGENCES	HEALTHY MUNCHIES
HOUSEHOLD	MEAL CHALLENGE

Write the words you need to hear. Repeat them to yourself.

Healthy Indulgence 5-minute recipe:

Strawberry Bruschetta

1. Toast slices of French bread or sourdough bread baguette under broiler.
2. While toasting make whipped goat cheese by mixing one large log of goat cheese and one 12 oz tub of whipped cream cheese
3. Add a bit of salt and pepper to whipped mixture
4. Slice strawberries. Thinner the better.

Spread whipped goat cheese on toasted bread and stack slices of strawberry on top.

Roll up 3 leaves of basil (like you would a cigar) and cut into ribbons with kitchen shears. You achieve ribbons by cutting the rolled-up basil vertically.

Drizzle with balsamic glaze (store bought works great)

Pro tip: Pour the glaze into a Ziplock bag and snip a very small hole in corner. Squeeze bag gently over the bruschetta. This will help the balsamic come out evenly on each piece.

<u>YOUR WEEKLY WHY</u>

Use this space to learn, grow and powerfully understand your thoughts and decision-making processes. Do this anytime you need clarity. Write it on a napkin, a back of an envelope, a journal, or anywhere you can write down and work through your thoughts.

The formula is simple.

Think of something during the week that excited you, upset you, stressed you out, made you inexplicably happy, or devastatingly sad. This could be an event, a choice, or even a conversation.

Then ask yourself WHY three times.

LIBERATION LETTER

Use this template to write a letter to someone or something you must release in order to move forward. This letter is meant for you to acknowledge the people, habits or activities that are no longer serving you. Use this template once a month to allow for optimal growth. Use this page or ideally a separate sheet of paper to allow for thoughtful responses.

Dear,

I am choosing to say goodbye because

You should know saying goodbye makes me feel

I now know that I

My inner voice is telling me

My values tell me

When I say goodbye to you I will no longer

Sincerely,

HELLO LETTER

Now that you have said goodbye to someone or something that has been holding you back from taking care of yourself and living abundantly, you must check in with yourself. This step is crucial as it will promote healing, create a plan to truly move forward and aid in closure. Use template once a month to allow for optimal growth. Use this page or ideally a separate sheet of paper or blank sheets in back of planner to allow for thoughtful responses.

Dear,

I just said goodbye to

Saying goodbye to makes me feel

but I know it is for the best. Some of the reasons I know this is for the best are because

Moving forward will be hard. That is ok. Please allow yourself time to feel

Some things you can do when you feel upset about closing this chapter are

Some people you can talk to are

There will be ups and downs, good days and bad days. That is part of difficult change, and it is normal and OK. On the really hard days a reminder you can use is

On the really great days a reminder you can use is

Here are three things I feel confident I can do to move forward and say goodbye

1.

2.

3.

Lastly, thank you for acknowledging it was time to let go. Thank you for honoring your health and your spirit. You deserve the best life has to offer and I am proud of you for putting yourself first.

Love always,

5 Minute Reflection

Mail

Write a letter to the person you were one month ago. What will that person learn by the end of the month? What experiences will be had? What obstacles will be overcome? How will that person have grown over the next 30 days?

"They can't hold us down if we stand up together"

-Katie Salzano

MY NEEDS THIS WEEK

Brainstorm your needs this week. Prioritize by number and add to your weekly calendar.

PERSONAL NEEDS:

PROFESSIONAL NEEDS:

SPIRITUAL NEEDS:

PHYSICAL NEEDS

EMOTIONAL NEEDS

PSYCHOLOGICAL NEEDS

IM POSSIBLE SELF WEEKLY SELF CARE PLAN

	MONDAY	TUESDAY	WEDNESDAY	THURSDAY	FRIDAY
PERSONAL					
PROFESSIONAL					
SPIRITUAL					
EMOTIONAL					
PHYSICAL					
PHYSICAL					

Reminders are personal mantras to be used in times of stress, decision-making, or in moments of gratitude and joy. Write your reminder for the week.

Support: Who or what will support you this week in your Self-Care goals.

REMINDERS	SUPPORT

Who has been your biggest supporter during your self-care journey so far? Write them a hand written letter of thanks. Everyone loves mail!

WEEKEND SELF CARE PLAN

PERSONAL	
PROFESSIONAL	
SPIRITUAL	
EMOTIONAL	
PHYSICAL	
PSYCHOLOGICAL	

Skin Care tip:

Next time you are at the store, pick up a bottle of Witch Hazel. If you are a mama, you might be familiar with Witch Hazel. This stuff was likely a miracle worker on post -partum swelling and aided in healing— Imagine what it can do for your face!

Witch Hazel can remedy acne, shrink pores, reduce swelling, uneven skin tone and dullness. It also is a superior cleanser to get any gunk your soap may have missed or residue it may have left.

WEEKLY SELF ESTEEM CHECK IN

Choose 1 of the following prompts to respond to for each day of the week

SOMETHING I MEDITATED ON	I FELT PROUD WHEN
SOMETHING I DID FOR SOMEONE ELSE	I LISTENED TO MY INNER VOICE WHEN
SOMETHING I DID FOR MYSELF	I FELT GOOD ABOUT MYSELF WHEN
I WAS HAPPY WHEN	I AM STARTING TO REALLY LIKE
I ACCOMPLISHED	I CHALLENGED MYSELF TO

MONDAY:

TUESDAY:

WEDNESDAY:

THURSDAY:

FRIDAY:

SATURDAY:

SUNDAY:

What changes do you want to see this week? What is one thing you can do to begin seeing that change?

SELF LOVE GROCERY LIST

As you create your grocery list for the week try to incorporate at least one food into each of the following categories to ensure you are taking care of your whole body, mind, and spirit. Plan your trips to the grocery store not just for food to eat but rather food that nourishes you. Under Meal Challenge-- think of a recipe you have been wanting to try, a food you want to cut out or add in to your diet. Do this weekly to see a drastic change in your overall health.

BRAIN FOOD	GUT HEALTH
SKIN AND HAIR CARE	**SLEEP**
HEALTHY INDULGENCES	**HEALTHY MUNCHIES**
HOUSEHOLD	**MEAL CHALLENGE**

Trouble sleeping?

Snack on tart cherries, almonds, bananas, Greek yogurt, or pour yourself a cup of chamomile tea

Tart Cherries are naturally high in melatonin; the hormone responsible for the sleep -awake cycle.

Almonds: Almonds are high in magnesium which promote sleep and muscle relaxation, Additionally, almonds are high in protein and this can help stabilize blood sugar levels which will not only help you fall asleep but stay asleep.

Bananas: Bananas are high in magnesium and potassium which help relaxation. Bananas are also great for easing cramps if your lack of sleep is due to over exertion at the gym or menstrual cycles.

YOUR WEEKLY WHY

Use this space to learn, grow and powerfully understand your thoughts and decision-making processes. Do this anytime you need clarity. Write it on a napkin, a back of an envelope, a journal, or anywhere you can write down and work through your thoughts.

The formula is simple.

Think of something during the week that excited you, upset you, stressed you out, made you inexplicably happy, or devastatingly sad. This could be an event, a choice, or even a conversation.

Then ask yourself WHY three times.

MY NEEDS THIS WEEK

Brainstorm your needs this week. Prioritize by number and add to your weekly calendar.

PERSONAL NEEDS:

PROFESSIONAL NEEDS:

SPIRITUAL NEEDS:

PHYSICAL NEEDS

EMOTIONAL NEEDS

PSYCHOLOGICAL NEEDS

IM POSSIBLE SELF WEEKLY SELF CARE PLAN

	MONDAY	TUESDAY	WEDNESDAY	THURSDAY	FRIDAY
PERSONAL					
PROFESSIONAL					
SPIRITUAL					
EMOTIONAL					
PHYSICAL					
PHYSICAL					

Reminders are personal mantras to be used in times of stress, decision-making, or in moments of gratitude and joy. Write your reminder for the week.

Support: Who or what will support you this week in your Self-Care goals.

REMINDERS	SUPPORT

In need of a new reminder?

Choose one from the list below:

"I trust myself; I believe in me; I am confident in my abilities."

"I am thankful for all that I have."

"I am in control of my thoughts, feelings and chooses."

"I am unstoppable."

"I give myself permission to succeed."

WEEKEND SELF CARE PLAN

PERSONAL	
PROFESSIONAL	
SPIRITUAL	
EMOTIONAL	
PHYSICAL	
PSYCHOLOGICAL	

What are your priorities today? How have they changed since you began using this guide?

WEEKLY SELF ESTEEM CHECK IN

Choose 1 of the following prompts to respond to for each day of the week

SOMETHING I DID WELL WAS	I FELT PROUD WHEN
SOMETHING I DID FOR SOMEONE ELSE	I TRIED
SOMETHING I DID FOR MYSELF	I FELT GOOD ABOUT MYSELF WHEN
I HAD A GOOD EXPERIENCE WITH	I LEARNED
I ACCOMPLISHED	I CHALLENGED MYSELF TO

MONDAY:

TUESDAY:

WEDNESDAY:

THURSDAY:

FRIDAY:

SATURDAY:

SUNDAY:

Gut Health Hack: Bone broth

- 2 lbs. bones
- 2 seconds of big glugs of Apple Cider Vinegar (you won't taste it. This is to break down the meat)
- 1 onion quartered or chopped. Larger to remove from broth, smaller if you don't mind eating them once broth is made.
- 2 carrots sliced
- 2 stalks of celery diced
- 1 bunch parsley chopped
- Salt & pepper
- Whole garlic head (press knife on the clove to squish it so flavor releases)
- Cover with water
- Bring to a boil
- Reduce to simmer for as many hours as possible. The longer the better. 8 is ideal.
- Pour into airtight mason jars

PRO TIP: Find brown or dark tinted mason jars. The broth will have some chunks in it from vegetables and beef cooking down. If that sort of thing is hard for you to see, go with a dark jar.

Try adding some cayenne for an added kick!

SELF LOVE GROCERY LIST

As you create your grocery list for the week try to incorporate at least one food into each of the following categories to ensure you are taking care of your whole body, mind, and spirit. Plan your trips to the grocery store not just for food to eat but rather food that nourishes you. Under Meal Challenge-- think of a recipe you have been wanting to try, a food you want to cut out or add in to your diet. Do this weekly to see a drastic change in your overall health.

BRAIN FOOD	GUT HEALTH
SKIN AND HAIR CARE	**SLEEP**
HEALTHY INDULGENCES	**HEALTHY MUNCHIES**
HOUSEHOLD	**MEAL CHALLENGE**

YOUR WEEKLY WHY

Use this space to learn, grow and powerfully understand your thoughts and decision-making processes. Do this anytime you need clarity. Write it on a napkin, a back of an envelope, a journal, or anywhere you can write down and work through your thoughts.

The formula is simple.

Think of something during the week that excited you, upset you, stressed you out, made you inexplicably happy, or devastatingly sad. This could be an event, a choice, or even a conversation.

Then ask yourself WHY three times.

MY NEEDS THIS WEEK

Brainstorm your needs this week. Prioritize by number and add to your weekly calendar.

PERSONAL NEEDS:

PROFESSIONAL NEEDS:

SPIRITUAL NEEDS:

PHYSICAL NEEDS

EMOTIONAL NEEDS

PSYCHOLOGICAL NEEDS

Quick! Give yourself a compliment!

IM POSSIBLE SELF WEEKLY SELF CARE PLAN

	MONDAY	TUESDAY	WEDNESDAY	THURSDAY	FRIDAY
PERSONAL					
PROFESSIONAL					
SPIRITUAL					
EMOTIONAL					
PHYSICAL					
PHYSICAL					

Reminders are personal mantras to be used in times of stress, decision-making, or in moments of gratitude and joy. Write your reminder for the week.

Support: Who or what will support you this week in your Self-Care goals.

REMINDERS	SUPPORT

Have you noticed any patterns in your Self-Care needs? Which need has required the most of your focus?

WEEKEND SELF CARE PLAN

PERSONAL	
PROFESSIONAL	
SPIRITUAL	
EMOTIONAL	
PHYSICAL	
PSYCHOLOGICAL	

What can you say to "No" to this week? What can you say "Yes" to?

WEEKLY SELF ESTEEM CHECK IN

Choose 3 of the following prompts to respond to for each day of the week

SOMETHING I DID WELL WAS	I FELT PROUD WHEN
SOMETHING I DID FOR SOMEONE ELSE	I TRIED
SOMETHING I DID FOR MYSELF	I FELT GOOD ABOUT MYSELF WHEN
I HAD A GOOD EXPERIENCE WITH	I LEARNED
I ACCOMPLISHED	I CHALLENGED MYSELF TO

MONDAY:

TUESDAY:

WEDNESDAY:

THURSDAY:

FRIDAY:

SATURDAY:

SUNDAY:

SELF LOVE GROCERY LIST

As you create your grocery list for the week try to incorporate at least one food into each of the following categories to ensure you are taking care of your whole body, mind, and spirit. Plan your trips to the grocery store not just for food to eat but rather food that nourishes you. Under Meal Challenge-- think of a recipe you have been wanting to try, a food you want to cut out or add in to your diet. Do this weekly to see a drastic change in your overall health.

BRAIN FOOD	GUT HEALTH
SKIN AND HAIR CARE	SLEEP
HEALTHY INDULGENCES	HEALTHY MUNCHIES
HOUSEHOLD	MEAL CHALLENGE

Are your meal choices supporting your self-care goals?

YOUR WEEKLY WHY

Use this space to learn, grow and powerfully understand your thoughts and decision-making processes. Do this anytime you need clarity. Write it on a napkin, a back of an envelope, a journal, or anywhere you can write down and work through your thoughts.

The formula is simple.

Think of something during the week that excited you, upset you, stressed you out, made you inexplicably happy, or devastatingly sad. This could be an event, a choice, or even a conversation.

Then ask yourself WHY three times.

MY NEEDS THIS WEEK

Brainstorm your needs this week. Prioritize by number and add to your weekly calendar.

PERSONAL NEEDS:

PROFESSIONAL NEEDS:

SPIRITUAL NEEDS:

PHYSICAL NEEDS

EMOTIONAL NEEDS

PSYCHOLOGICAL NEEDS

IM POSSIBLE SELF WEEKLY SELF CARE PLAN

	MONDAY	TUESDAY	WEDNESDAY	THURSDAY	FRIDAY
PERSONAL					
PROFESSIONAL					
SPIRITUAL					
EMOTIONAL					
PHYSICAL					
PHYSICAL					

Reminders are personal mantras to be used in times of stress, decision-making, or in moments of gratitude and joy. Write your reminder for the week.

Support: Who or what will support you this week in your Self-Care goals.

REMINDERS	SUPPORT

What is one thing you can do for yourself today?

WEEKEND SELF CARE PLAN

PERSONAL	
PROFESSIONAL	
SPIRITUAL	
EMOTIONAL	
PHYSICAL	
PSYCHOLOGICAL	

Journal Prompt:

How are you progressing with your Self-Care goals? What have you noticed?

WEEKLY SELF ESTEEM CHECK IN

Choose 1 of the following prompts to respond to for each day of the week

SOMETHING I LIKE ABOUT MYSELF	I FELT PROUD WHEN
SOMETHING I DID FOR SOMEONE ELSE	I PAID A COMPLIMENT TO
SOMETHING I DID FOR MYSELF	I FELT GOOD ABOUT MYSELF WHEN
I HAD A GOOD EXPERIENCE WITH	I TRUSTED
I ACCOMPLISHED	I CHALLENGED MYSELF TO

MONDAY:

TUESDAY:

WEDNESDAY:

THURSDAY:

FRIDAY:

SATURDAY:

SUNDAY:

SELF LOVE GROCERY LIST

As you create your grocery list for the week try to incorporate at least one food into each of the following categories to ensure you are taking care of your whole body, mind, and spirit. Plan your trips to the grocery store not just for food to eat but rather food that nourishes you. Under Meal Challenge-- think of a recipe you have been wanting to try, a food you want to cut out or add in to your diet. Do this weekly to see a drastic change in your overall health.

BRAIN FOOD	GUT HEALTH
SKIN AND HAIR CARE	SLEEP
HEALTHY INDULGENCES	HEALTHY MUNCHIES
HOUSEHOLD	MEAL CHALLENGE

YOUR WEEKLY WHY

Use this space to learn, grow and powerfully understand your thoughts and decision-making processes. Do this anytime you need clarity. Write it on a napkin, a back of an envelope, a journal, or anywhere you can write down and work through your thoughts.

The formula is simple.

Think of something during the week that excited you, upset you, stressed you out, made you inexplicably happy, or devastatingly sad. This could be an event, a choice, or even a conversation.

Then ask yourself WHY three times.

5 Minute Reflection

Feed Me

What healthy foods did you enjoy this month?

How did eating healthy make you feel?

What unhealthy foods did you eat this month?

How did eating unhealthy make you feel?

What people, events or feelings influenced your meal choices?

How would you like to eat next month? Are there any foods you want to try?

BEHAVIOR CHANGE PLANNING

This activity will require you to be honest with yourself. Think of a behavior or habit you would like to change. This could be BIG, like negative thinking, obsessing, partying too much, gravitating towards toxic relationships, or it could be smaller like interrupting, being forgetful, or running self into ground. Choose a behavior and attack.

What behavior do I want to change?

What could happen if I no longer do this behavior?

How will my life be different without this behavior?

What are three ways I can start preparing myself to make this change?

Who can I (IF ANYONE) ask to help me with this change?

When will I start? (EXACT DATE)

How will I know I am making progress with this change?

What do I imagine my life will be like when I make this change?

TAKE A LOOK BACK

Congratulations! You have completed the IM POSSIBLE Self Care Planning Guide. Let's take a look back at what you have learned about yourself.

What have you learned about yourself?

What was the most common self -care theme?

What goals did you achieve for yourself this year?

What changes have you noticed in your life since beginning the planner?

LET'S TAKE A LOOK AT YOUR CUPS

Just as you did in the beginning of this guide, take a look at what is filing your cups now that you have completed a year of dedicated self -care. After you fill out the worksheet go back to the beginning and take note of what has changed.

There are six elements of self-care.

PHYSICAL: Movement. Nutrition. Health.

PERSONAL: Relationships with self and others

SPIRITUAL: Listening to an inner voice and universe.

EMOTIONAL: Mindfulness and positive Self Talk

PROFESSIONAL: Work/Life balance.

PSYCHOLOGICAL: Self Reflection & Self Awareness

What Is in My Cup

PROFFESIONAL	
PERSONAL	
SPIRITUAL	
PHYSICAL	
PSYCHOLOGICAL	
EMOTIONAL	

"This is your reminder to celebrate the small WINS along the way. These are just as important as the mountaintop wins. Big or small, acknowledge them all. Acknowledge the goodness happening on your journey."

-Sarah Patton

Made in the USA
Middletown, DE
03 January 2023

21283140R00258